Spiritual Gifts

A Manual Inspired by the Holy Spirit for the purpose of Equipping and Training the Church

Myra Armstrong

A Voice for God

Copyright © 2024 Myra Armstrong

All rights reserved. No portion of this book may be reproduced in any form without written permission from the publisher or author, except as permitted by U.S. copyright law, except for the use of brief quotations in a book review.

Scripture taken from the New King James Version®. Copyright © 1982 by Thomas Nelson. Used by permission. All rights reserved.

Holy Bible, New Living Translation, Copyright © 1996, 2004, 2015 by Tyndale House Foundation. Used by permission of Tyndale House Publishers, Inc., Carol Stream, Illinois 60188. All rights reserved.

ISBN Paperback 978-1-953473-25-7

Library of Congress Control Number: 2024949296

Purple Pearls Publishing,
PO Box 293
Oceano, California 93475

Cover design: Laura Gaisie
Developmental Editor: Tim Osuch

Printed in the United States of America

Contents

Introduction	1
Session 1 - *God Wants to Communicate*	3
Session 2 - *Discerning the Voice of God*	15
Session 3 – *Ministering the Mind of Christ*	25
Session 4 – *The Revelation Gifts*	35
Session 5 – *The Inspirational Gifts*	59
Session 6 – *The Power Gifts*	63
Session 7 – *The Keys to the Kingdom*	69
Session 8 – *Why is Prophesy for Today?*	85
Session 9 – *Developing Prophetic Teams*	101
Session 10 – *What is a Prophetic Burden*	109
Index	115
In My Words	119

Introduction

The purpose of the gifts of the spirit is for today and the edification of the body of Christ. We are the extended parts of His body, and He delights in us to demonstrate His existence, power, and purpose for all those who love and seek Him earnestly through His Holy Spirit. The Holy Spirit enables us and empowers us to operate in the gifts of the spirit with effectiveness with His gracefulness or graciousness and to operate through the love of God.

In this book, you will learn that a spiritual gift is a God-given ability, distributed to individual Christians, by Holy Spirit. This gift allows you to operate in God's mission and is intended in every believer's life to execute God's mission and His purpose for your life.

Key Points:

1. You will learn the difference between spiritual gifts and natural talents. You will learn that physical abilities and strengths, artistic and musical skills, athletic capabilities, and more, are best described as talents.

2. Spiritual gifts are just that, spiritual and not natural. They can only be accessed through the Holy Spirit to empower believers with supernatural abilities to experience and operate in a fashion that exceeds that found in the natural world. For example, to speak or sing in an unknown language, to heal the sick, to speak words of God with His power of agreement.

3. You will learn that spiritual gifts are not the best sign of spirituality. Indeed, you will know that Christ-like maturity is primarily indicated by the manifestation of the fruit of the Spirit, and not by the presence of spiritual gifts.

4. From this manual, you will know the gifts of The Spirit, how to identify them, and how to walk in them.

SESSION 1: God Wants To Communicate

Key Verse: Exodus 20:22 (NLT)
22 And the LORD said to Moses, "Say this to the people of Israel: You saw for yourselves that I spoke to you from heaven.

The Purpose: God is a communicative God, and that dialogue is a part of His nature. The benefits of hearing will seed expectation. These will instill fresh faith and confidence that God is speaking to the individual believer and that each one of us is designed to hear. God is the creator, sustainer, redeemer, and judge. We relate to these parts of who He is by interacting with Him by His Spirit. The more we desire to know Him, the more He will make Himself known to us. It starts with intimacy with Him. Spend time in His word and/or spend time with Him yielding in prayer. Have you ever thought to ask Him how He is doing, or what is on His heart. Well, folks, it starts there. How can you ever get to know anything or anyone without interaction?

> Ezekiel 3:22 (NLT) Then the LORD took hold of me and said, "Get up and go out into the valley, and I will speak to you there."

(Additional scriptures: Genesis 1:3, Exodus 33:11, Psalm 50:1, 1 Corinthians 15:1-4, Hebrews 1:3)

I. WHY GOD WANTS TO COMMUNICATE:

- **God desires to communicate His desires, plans, and purposes**

SESSION 1: God Wants to Communicate

> Jeremiah 29:11 (NLT) *For I know the plans I have for you, says the LORD. They are plans for good and not for disaster, to give you a future and a hope.*

- **God is relational:**

    > 1 John 4:16 (NLT) *We know how much God loves us, and we have put our trust in his love. God is love, and all who live in love live in God, and God lives in them.*

A. IT IS COMMON FOR GOD TO COMMUNICATE

From Genesis chapters 1, 2, and 3 God is communicating with man. Also, in Ezekiel and Jeremiah.

B. Hearing the voice of the Lord brings us many benefits

1) <u>It brings intimacy</u>

> John 15:15-16 (NLT) *I no longer call you slaves, because a master doesn't confide in his slaves. Now you are my friends, since I have told you everything the Father told me.* **16** *You didn't choose me. I chose you. I appointed you to go and produce lasting fruit, so that the Father will give you whatever you ask for, using my name.*

2) <u>It brings peace in our hearts</u>

His voice comforts and encourages us during trials and adversity. He gives the wisdom to walk through a transition. His voice brings unity and purpose to our corporate existence: We discover His divine purpose and destiny.

3) *It brings revelation of His plan for us*

His voice reveals strategies, direction, and wisdom to conduct our lives.

4) *It brings protection to our lives*

Psalm 91:14-15 (NLT) *The Lord says, "I will rescue those who love me. I will protect those who trust in my name. 15 When they call on me, I will answer; I will be with them in trouble. I will rescue and honor them.*

John 10:1-2 (NLT) *I tell you the truth, anyone who sneaks over the wall of a sheepfold, rather than going through the gate, must surely be a thief and a robber! 2 But the one who enters through the gate is the shepherd of the sheep.*

(My thoughts are the sheepfolds were caves, sheds, or pen areas surrounded by walls and the shepherd often slept lying across the doorway to protect the sheep. Jesus is the good shepherd.)

5) *It brings provision*

He positions us to prosper. Joshua 1:6-8 (NLT) *6 Be strong and courageous, for you are the one who will lead these people to possess all the land I swore to their ancestors I would give them. 7 Be strong and very courageous. Be careful to obey all the instructions Moses gave you. Do not deviate from them, turning either to the right or to the left. Then you will be successful in everything you do. 8 Study this book of instruction continually. Meditate on it day and night*

SESSION 1: God Wants to Communicate

> *so you will be sure to obey everything written in it. Only then will you prosper and succeed in all you do.*

6) **It brings corrective transformation**
Communication brings reformation from the inside out.

> Romans 8:29-30 *For God knew his people in advance, and he chose them to become like his Son so that his Son would be the firstborn among many brothers and sisters. 30 And having chosen them, he called them to come to him. And having called them, he gave them right standing with himself. And having given them right standing, he gave them his glory.*

He is continually and eternally speaking to mankind. Jesus' sheep recognize His voice. John 10:27-28 and John 10:3-5 speak to this. A person's voice conveys more than words, it conveys intent.

Sometimes it speaks of warmth, comfort, and encouragement. Sometimes it provides us with warmth. Shepherds in ancient times in the Middle East were known for calling their sheep by name and each sheep would respond to its own name. Jesus knows your name, hear His call.

John 10:27-28 (NLT) *My sheep listen to my voice; I know them, and they follow me. 28 I give them eternal life, and they will never perish. No one can snatch them away from me.*

John 10:3-5 (NLT) *The gatekeeper opens the gate for him, and the sheep recognize his voice and come to him. He calls his own sheep by name and leads them out. 4 After he has gathered his own flock, he walks ahead of them, and they follow him because they know his voice. 5 They won't follow a stranger; they will run from him because they don't know his voice.*

II. METHODS OF COMMUNICATION

Ever since sin dulled man's ability to hear God's voice, He has chosen other means of communication.

A. OLD TESTAMENT PROPHETS - God's communication channels

Prophets revealed in the Old Testament are referred to as **major prophets and minor prophets.**

- **Major Prophets:** Isaiah, Jeremiah, the writer of Lamentations (thought to be Jeremiah), Ezekiel, and Daniel.
- **Minor Prophets:** Hosea, Joel, Amos, Obadiah, Jonah, Micah, Nahum, Habakkuk, Zephaniah, Haggai, Zechariah, and Malachi.

Major Prophets wrote the longest books of prophecy and Minor Prophets wrote the shorter books of prophecy. There were also female Prophetesses. All of the books of the prophets are of male prophets, however, there were at least four Prophetesses in the Old Testament. The two most prominent are Miriam, the sister of Moses, and Deborah a Judge and also referred to as a Prophetess, (See Exodus 15:20 and Judges 4:4).

B. JESUS – GOD'S ULTIMATE REVEALER

Jesus Christ is the brightest display of God's glory and the greatest expression of God's person ever to occur in eternity. The verbal and visual manifestation of God's own thoughts, words, principles and pattern of living. Jesus' redemptive act removed the cause of our dullness in hearing God, (Romans 11:7-8 NLT).

C. THE BIBLE / HISTORY – GOD IN WRITTEN FORM

The mind, the will, and the purposes of God. Scripture is the complete written revelation of God.

D. THE HOLY SPIRIT – God's voice, teacher, and agent of truth and our comforter

God's voice in and within us, to lead us into all Truth. A key to hearing God's direction is through the amplifying and clarifying voice of the Holy Spirit. The Holy Spirit speaks directly to the heart of all who believe in Him, and confess His existence as the third person of the Trinity.

E. THE PROPHET – GOD'S SPOKESMAN

A Prophet is a special agent to deliver God's message. That special voice that brings illumination about what is already written without additions or subtractions, and without contradictions. Those called and exercised to recognize God's voice and express His thoughts are for the edifying of the body and building of the Church in this hour. One who is called to the *office of a Prophet* is called to oversee Prophets and to train and equip the next generation of Prophets to build up the Church.

1. A Prophet points and directs
2. As well as confronts and provokes in order to help leaders make significant decisions in the Church.

1 Corinthians 14:3 (NLT) *But one who prophesies strengthens others, encourages them, and comforts them.*

1 Thessalonians 5:20-21 (NLT) *Do not scoff at prophecies, 21 but test everything that is said.*

F. PROPHECY – THE VOICE OF THE HOLY SPIRIT

Acts 2:17 (NLT) *In the last days, God says, "I will pour out my spirit upon all people. Your sons and daughters will prophesy. Your young men will see visions, and your old men will dream dreams.*

1 Corinthians 12:4-11 (NLT) *There are different kinds of spiritual gifts, but the same Spirit is the source of them all. 5 There are different kinds of service, but we serve the same Lord. 6 God works in different ways, but it is the same God who does the work in all of us. 7 A spiritual gift is given to each of us so we can help each other. 8 To one person the Spirit gives the ability to give wise advice; to another the same Spirit gives a message of special knowledge. 9 The same Spirit gives great faith to another, and to someone else the Spirit gives the gift of healing. 10 He gives one person the power to perform miracles, and another the ability to prophesy. He gives someone else the ability to discern whether a message is from the Spirit of God or from another spirit. Still another person is given the ability to speak in unknown languages, while another is given the ability to interpret what is being said. 11 It is the one and only Spirit who distributes all these gifts. He alone decides which gift each person should have.*

2 Peter 1:19-21 (NLT) *Because of that experience, we have even greater confidence in the message proclaimed by the prophets. You must pay close attention to what they wrote, for their words are like a lamp shining in a dark place—until the Day dawns, and Christ the Morning Star shines in your hearts. 20 Above all, you must realize that no prophecy in Scripture ever came from the prophet's own understanding, 21 or from human initiative. No,*

> *those prophets were moved by the Holy Spirit, and they spoke from God.*

It reveals the mind of Christ to humanity. It never contradicts His Word. He will never lie nor deny himself.

- **Covet to prophesy**. God wants His will to be vocalized. We must cultivate a desire in our own hearts to prophesy for the purpose of serving others.

- To **covet** something is to strongly yearn to possess or to have that thing.

    > 1 Corinthians 14:39 (NLT) *So, my dear brothers and sisters, be eager to prophesy, and don't forbid speaking in tongues.*

To prophesy means to give and confirm specific instructions to individuals concerning His will for their lives.

1. It is a doorway to merge other gifts of the Holy Spirit in the individual and in the body.

2. Prophecy is never a substitute for an individual's responsibility and privilege to hear God's voice.

3. God wants intimacy on a personal level with each individual.

4. The revelatory mind of God is a supernatural word of inspiration from God, and it is the heart of God.

5. Prayer can and will access the mind and heart of God.

G. ANGELS – THE MESSENGERS OF GOD

Hebrews 1:13-14 (NLT) *And God never said to any of the angels, "sit in the place of honor at my right hand until I humble your enemies, making them a footstool under your feet. 14 Therefore, angels are only servants – spirits sent to care for people who will inherit salvation.*

- **Angels are God's messengers**. They are spiritual beings created by God and are under His authority. They have several functions:

    1. Serving believers
    2. Protecting the helpless
    3. Proclaiming God's message

We must remember that angels administer God's care. They are not to be worshiped or prayed to, but they serve God and carry out His purposes and God will use them to care for those who we love.

Matthew 18:10 (NLT) *Beware that you don't look down on any of these little ones. For I tell you that in heaven their angels are always in the presence of my heavenly Father.*

III. GOD CREATED US TO HEAR HIS VOICE

Proverbs 20:12 (NLT) *Ears to hear and eyes to see- both are gifts from the Lord.*

God made our ears to hear. In order to hear God we need to listen. Listening can be challenging to our human mind as our natural mind can be distracting which may dull our hearing of the Lord. His voice can be confused in our minds with our thoughts. That is why we must

SESSION 1: God Wants to Communicate

desire to focus on God's thoughts, with our hearts being aligned with His, as well as aligning with His own words, meaning scripture. That is His own language "Logos" written word of God.

> Colossians 3:1-2 (NLT) *Since you have been raised to new life with Christ, set your sights on the realities of heaven, where Christ sits at God's right hand. 2 Think about the things of heaven, not the things of earth.*

This is not based on our righteousness. The effects of sin can hinder our hearing God. He desires to communicate, so desire to hear Him! Yes prayer, in fact, much prayer is essential to begin with.

Key Point: Repentance and sanctification is necessary at all times in the purity of hearing from God.

There is a conversational aspect to God's communication

> Genesis 3:8-10 (NLT) *When the cool evening breezes were blowing, the man and his wife heard the Lord God walking about in the garden. So they hid from the Lord God among the trees. 9 Then the Lord God called to the man, "Where are you?" 10 He replied, "I heard you walking in the garden, so I hid. I was afraid because I was naked."*

- **God speaking to man was not uncommon**

Ezekiel 2:1-3 (NLT) *"Stand up, son of man," said the voice. "I want to speak with you." 2 The Spirit came into me as he spoke, and he set me on my feet. I listened carefully to his words. 3 "Son of man," he said, "I am sending you to the nation Israel, a rebellious nation that has rebelled against me. They and their ancestors have been rebelling against me to this very day."*

- **He still desires dialogue**

    Relationships require dialogue, so does intimacy.

    Psalm 37:4 (NLT) *Take delight in the Lord, and he will give you your heart's desires.*

True delight in Him causes us to focus our sights on what matters to Him and to seek what He longs for; What's His pleasure, what pleases Him and what are His desires?

SESSION 1: God Wants to Communicate

SESSION 2: Discerning the Voice of God

Key Verse: 1 Timothy 1:18-19 (NLT)
18 Timothy, my son, here are my instructions for you, based on the prophetic words spoken about you earlier. May they help you fight well in the Lord's battle. 19 Cling to your faith in Christ, and keep your conscience clear. For some people have deliberately violated their consciences; as a result, their faith has been shipwrecked.

The Purpose: To explore the various ways God speaks to believers today, with special emphasis on how God speaks personally to them. The believer will be able to identify how God created them to receive, (visually, audibly, or sensing). There will be a greater appreciation of how others receive from God. In my experience in the prophetic, I would also include the five natural senses that God in His creative nature chooses to use for His creation. This is what I find amazing about our God, He is full of mystery, miracles, signs, and wonders.

1. Touch
2. Smell
3. Hearing
4. Sight
5. Taste

God uses all of these and accesses them from the supernatural realm where He operates. What does a Realm mean: **A realm is between heaven and earth.** There are three heavenly realms. *(Eph. 2:2), (Dan. 10:13), (2 Cor. 12:2) (NKJV)*

- The **First Heaven** is the ***Earthly Realm*** where we live and birds fly. This is the A*tmospheric* heaven where Satan dwells, the prince of the power of the air.

SESSION 2: Discerning the Voice of God

- The **Second Heaven** is the *Celestial Realm*, where angelic wars and battles are fought on our behalf. This is also where Satan first fell, and where demons are now fighting. *Rev. 12:4-12, 14:6,7 (NKJV)*
- The **Third Heaven** is the *Throne Room Of God*. This is where God dwells, the Throne room. *2 Cor. 12:2-4 (NKJV)*

These three realms are between heaven and earth, and God accesses the natural realm of earth from the supernatural realm of heaven (a realm is between heaven and earth).

1. The Realm of the Spirit is a place where believers connect with God.
2. The Heavenly Realm encompasses all spirit beings and where angelic and demonic activity takes place.
3. The Kingdom of God is a spiritual realm over which God reigns as King or the fulfillment on the earth of God's will.

I. LEARNING TO DISCERN GOD'S VOICE

A. Discernment comes as a process of growth

Continue to exercise by connecting with Jesus through the Holy Spirit on a continual basis so He can begin to trust you with this gift. Don't concentrate too much on reason or human analysis. Its effectiveness is spiritually activated by growing in hearing God's voice (as you seek Him in prayer) asking Him to develop this gift for His glory and pouring out His Spirit and anointing this gift in you. You need to spend time with the Father and extend faith to hear Him. *"My sheep hear my voice,"* (John 10:27).

Learn to turn on, tune in, and control the volume. Avoid distractions when God is talking to you. For example, ask the Holy Spirit to shut off your thoughts that are human and not spirit. No phones on, no television, or music. At least this was helpful when the Holy Spirit trained me. There will also be a lot of wilderness time, meaning when there are very little natural things to cause distraction. God wants to invade your thoughts with His thoughts, Amen.

Walk it out until there is possession and ownership, then stewardship. Be very patient with the Holy Spirit as He teaches you. Pay close attention, expecting, and expecting. God graces those who care for the things that He cares for. Allow the Holy Spirit to build within you the assurances and confidence that come from Him. He is the one who empowers the gifts. We don't want to be ignorant of the devices of the enemy. The gift of discernment is a beautiful gift essentially because you, over time, receive a lot of God's revelation wisdom of what He reveals to you that others cannot see, for the protection of the Church and you. Remember that Satan uses many disguises.

B. God speaks differently to every person

There are three primary methods:

1. Mental images or pictures

Revelation 1:16-20 (NLT) *He held seven stars in his right hand, and a sharp two-edged sword came from his mouth. And his face was like the sun in all its brilliance. 17 When I saw him, I fell at his feet as if I were dead. But he laid his right hand on me and said, "Don't be afraid! I am the First and the Last. 18 I am the living one. I died, but look – I am alive forever and ever! And I hold the keys of death and the grave. 19 Write down what you have seen – both the things that are now happening and the things that will happen. 20 This is the meaning of the mystery of the seven stars you saw in my right hand and the seven gold lampstands: The seven stars are the angels of the seven churches, and the seven lampstands are the seven churches.*

SESSION 2: Discerning the Voice of God

2. **Physical sensations and heartfelt impressions of God's emotions of love**

Jeremiah 4:5-8 (NLT) *"Shout to Judah, and broadcast to Jerusalem! Tell them to sound the alarm throughout the land: "Run for your lives! Flee to the fortified cities!"* 6 *Raise a signal flag as a warning for Jerusalem: Flee now! Do not delay!" For I am bringing terrible destruction upon you from the north."* 7 *A lion stalks from its den, a destroyer of nations. It has left its lair and is headed your way. It's going to devastate your land! Your towns will lie in ruins, with no one living in them anymore.* 8 *So put on clothes of mourning and weep with broken hearts, for the fierce anger of the Lord is upon us.*

Ezekiel 3:1-3 (NLT) *The voice said to me, "Son of man, eat what I am giving you – eat this scroll! Then go and give its message to the people of Israel."* 2 *So I opened my mouth, and he fed me the scroll.* 3 *He said to me, "Son of man, feed your stomach and fill your body with this scroll which I am giving you." Then I ate it, and it was sweet as honey in my mouth.*

Ezekiel 1:1 (NLT) *On July 31 of my thirtieth year, while I was with the Judean exiles beside the Kebar River in Babylon, the heavens were opened and I saw visions of God.*

3. **Hearing words, or words in thought form**

Jeremiah 1:9-10 (NLT) *Then the Lord reached out and touched my mouth and said, Look, I have put my words in your mouth!* 10 *Today I appoint you to stand up against nations and kingdoms. Some you must uproot and tear down, destroy and overthrow. Others you must build up and plant."*

In Acts 9:4, Paul heard a voice on the day of his conversion. In Acts 10, Cornelius and Peter received instruction from the Lord through visions. In Genesis 37, Joseph had a dream.

C. Learn to discern

Each one of us has a primary way – a similar fashion in which we hear the voice of the Lord repeatedly. The process is understood within the choices to activate, exercise, and measure hearing God's voice. Like a police scanner, we don't all hear His voice on the same frequency. We have to allow the Holy Spirit to fine-tune us, by asking the Holy Spirit to bring clarity regarding His thoughts. Do not limit God. In time God may use other ways to speak to us. Be sensitive. Also, be quiet and listen. Prayer is sometimes in silence.

II. THREE PRIMARY WAYS GOD COMMUNICATES

1. By Seeing

Jeremiah 1:13-15 (NLT) *Then the Lord spoke to me again and asked, "What do you see now?" And I replied, "I see a pot of boiling water, spilling from the north." 14 "Yes," the Lord said, "for terror from the north will boil out on the people of this land. 15 Listen! I am calling the armies of the kingdoms of the north to come to Jerusalem. I the Lord have spoken!"*

a. **The Seer Gift or Mental images** - An instantaneous mental picture that can be described in much detail, or an example often happens when in the flow of prophesying over someone.

b. **Visions** - Supernatural occurrences where the Lord opens the natural eyes to see into the spiritual realm.

SESSION 2: Discerning the Voice of God

> Revelation 1:10-12 (NLT) *It was the Lord's Day, and I was worshiping in the Spirit. Suddenly, I heard behind me a loud voice like a trumpet blast. 11 It said, "Write in a book everything you see, and send it to the seven churches in the cities of Ephesus, Smyrna, Pergamum, Thyatira, Sardis, Philadelphia, and Laodicea." 12 When I turned to see who was speaking to me, I saw seven gold lampstands.*

> Revelation 4:1-2 (NLT) *Then as I looked, I saw a door standing open in heaven, and the same voice I heard before spoke to me like a trumpet blast. The voice said, "Come up here, and I will show you what must happen after this." 2 And instantly I was in the Spirit, and I saw a throne in heaven and someone sitting on it.*

> Revelations 21:10-11 (NLT) *So he took me in the Spirit to a great, high mountain, and he showed me the holy city, Jerusalem, descending out of heaven from God. 11 It shone with the glory of God and sparkled like a precious stone – like jasper as clear as crystal.*

c. **Dreams** (night visions)

> Joel 2:28 (NLT) *Then, after doing all those things, I will pour out my Spirit upon all people. Your sons and daughters will prophesy. Your old men with dream dreams, and your young men will see visions.*

> Daniel 7:2 (NLT) *In my vision that night, I, Daniel, saw a great storm churning the surface of a great sea, with strong winds blowing from every direction.*

2. By Hearing

Proverbs 20:12 (NLT) *Ears to hear and eyes to see – both are gifts from the Lord.*

- **Hearing comes by:**

1) An audible voice to the ear
2) More often a strong mental thought from the Holy Spirit to our human spirit.
3) A slight impression, to make His impression, which you may quickly dismiss. Back up!
4) The still small voice

1 Kings 19:11-13 (NLT) *"Go out and stand before me on the mountain, "the Lord told him. And as Elijah stood there, the Lord passed by, and a mighty windstorm hit the mountain. It was such a terrible blast that the rocks were torn loose, but the Lord was not in the wind. After the wind there was an earthquake, but the Lord was not in the earthquake. 12 And after the earthquake there was a fire, but the Lord was not in the fire. And after the fire there was the sound of a gentle whisper. 13 When Elijah heard it, he wrapped his face in his cloak and went out and stood at the entrance of the cave. And a voice said, "What are you doing here, Elijah?"*

Isaiah 30:21 (NLT) *Your own ears will hear him. Right behind you a voice will say, "This is the way you should go," whether to the right or to the left.*

SESSION 2: Discerning the Voice of God

- **KEYS TO REMEMBER**

  Prayer is the main key. How I learned to discern His voice is through prayer.

- <u>*Sounds like your own voice*</u> - His voice always precedes expectation, but I'd actually hear myself, which is communication with God in the first voice.

- <u>*Learn to listen*</u> - It is a skill. When you desire to be skilled at something put it into practice. Meaning if you desire to be skilled at something, put it into use. Sit quietly and be patient with the Holy Spirit. When you are able to be still and listen, you will now be able to hear His voice of instruction. Upon applying these principles consistently, you will attain an ear to hear God clearly.

- <u>*Remain teachable*</u> - He, the Holy Spirit, wants to teach you. Remember, the Holy Spirit is the Helper. Always ask Him to continually teach you. A teachable spirit comes with a passion for learning and wanting to be open to the unusual ways He operates to get your attention when you're not listening. When you are not listening there will be mistakes which will help you learn more diligently. Don't give up, a teachable person will be persistent in seeking the Holy Spirit's direction. When I would go blank, I would often be distracted by peripheral, human thoughts.

- <u>*Look for the "thought" behind the thought*</u> - which often comes very quickly and is easily overlooked or erased while looking for something more complicated. His voice will oftentimes resonate with His word, His nature as God, and His mind (attitude).

3. Impressions or sensing:

Matthew 9:36 (NLT) When he saw the crowds, he had compassion on them because they were confused and helpless, like sheep without a shepherd.

   a. **An emotion felt**. At times an overwhelming compassion. At times an overwhelming sadness like weeping, even at times seemingly for no apparent reason.

   b. **A deep inward knowing** about a situation, person, etc. Especially when you are praying for folks.

   c. **Follow peace**. Accompanied with His "joy" and assuredness, an unexplainable experience.

SESSION 2: Discerning the Voice of God

SESSION 3: Ministering the Mind of Christ

Key Verse: Romans 8:5-6 (NLT)

5 Those who are dominated by the sinful nature think about sinful things, but those who are controlled by the Holy Spirit think about things that please The Spirit. 6 So letting your sinful nature control your mind leads to death. But letting the Spirit control your mind leads to life and peace.

The Purpose: The Holy Spirit allows us to make a connection with the mind of God. The Holy Spirit also aids the believer to connect with His desires first through different sources; desire, thought, impression, and motivation. Also, to connect our understanding which in turn yields awareness, confident understanding discerning God's thoughts from the throne room.

Philippians 2:5 (NLT) *You must have the same attitude that Christ Jesus had.*

- Right thinking produces the right actions.
- Our actions are the fruit of our deepest thoughts.

I. THE FIVE SCRIPTURAL MINDS

1. **_The Spiritual mind_** (defined as)

   a) The mind of every born-again Spirit-filled believer.

SESSION 3: Ministering the Mind of Christ

> 1 Corinthians 2:16 (NLT) *For, who can know the Lord's thoughts? Who knows enough to teach him?" But we understand these things, for we have the mind of Christ.*

The spiritual mind must characterize the attribute of the thoughts originating from Christ in agreement with the Word.

   b) The spiritual mind functions in divinely inspired thoughts, not thoughts based upon one's doctrine, attitude, education, or religion.

   c) The spiritual mind is controlled by the fruit of the Holy Spirit.

> Galatians 5:22-23 (NLT) *But the Holy Spirit produces this kind of fruit in our lives: love, joy, peace, patience, kindness, goodness, faithfulness, 23 gentleness, and self-control. There is no law against these things.*

   d) The spiritual mind is a mind in which Kingdom principles prevail.

> Philippians 4:8 (NLT) *And now, dear brothers and sisters, one final thing. Fix your thoughts on what is true, honorable, and right, and pure, and lovely, and admirable. Think on these things that are excellent and worthy of praise.*

The gift of the Spirit should operate through these Godly principles.

2. *The Soulish mind* (defined as)

> 1 Corinthians 10:5-7 (NLT) *Yet God was not pleased with most of them, and their bodies were scattered in the wilderness. 6 These things happened as a warning to us, so that we would not crave evil things as they did, 7 or worship*

idols as some of them did. As the Scriptures say, "The people celebrated with feasting and drinking, and they indulged in pagan revelry."

Key Point: The soulish mind is a combination of the mind, will, and emotions. The soulish mind is:

a. A combination of natural and spiritual
b. Imagination produces self-motivated ideas, plans, and strategies, which are not automatically God's ideas.
c. The ability to perceive beyond what evidence reveals – a soulish sensitivity, intuition, or psychic abilities.
d. Is self-serving.
e. The mind that tries to control and direct while ministering, is also self-serving.
f. The mind that tries to operate on biblical knowledge without a spiritual mind.
g. The mind that tries to manipulate divine things for selfish purposes. For example, Simon the sorcerer in Acts 8:9-24.
h. That which uses and manipulates others by using spiritual abilities through the disguise of a prophecy or word from God. It operates in self-righteousness. Giving false prophecy by prophesying to a person's own desires versus what God's truth is. Appealing to the human heart and feeling of the person versus speaking God's truth.

3. ### *The Natural mind*

   Genesis 2:7 (NLT) *Then the Lord God formed man from the dust of the ground. He breathed the breath of life into the man's nostrils, and the man became a living person.*

   a. The natural mind produces normal thoughts that are neither good nor bad.

SESSION 3: Ministering the Mind of Christ

      b. Is trained, skilled, and educated for natural things.

      c. It gives the ability to live and function, to do daily things.

      d. It is the control center of the human body.

      e. It will also boast in their achievements and natural abilities as though they were the originators.

4. *The Carnal mind*

Romans 8:6-7 (KJV) *For to be carnally minded is death; but to be spiritually minded is life and peace. 7 Because the carnal mind is enmity against God: for it is not subject to the law of God, neither indeed can be.*

Enmity: means the state of feeling actively hostile to someone or something, as against God. Carnal-minded seem spiritual but have mechanical behaviors that are lifeless and dull, a form of Godliness but denying the power thereof. It is consumed with carnal thoughts and desires. So, letting sinful nature control your mind leads to death. But letting the Spirit control your mind leads to a life of peace.

1 Corinthians 3:3 (NLT) *for you are still controlled by your sinful nature. You are jealous of one another and quarrel with each other. Doesn't that prove you are controlled by your sinful nature? Aren't you living like people of the world?*

- The carnal mind is exemplified by:

      a. Thoughts that originate from the lust of the flesh, the lust of the eyes, and the pride of life.

b. Thoughts that identify with and promote the works of the flesh.

> Galatians 5:19-21 (NLT) *When you follow the desires of your sinful nature, the results are very clear: sexual immorality, impurity, lustful pleasures, 20 idolatry, sorcery, hostility, quarreling, jealousy, outbursts of anger, selfish ambition, dissension, division, 21 envy, drunkenness, wild parties, and other sins like these. Let me tell you again, as I have before, that anyone living that sort of life will not inherit the Kingdom of God.*

c. Being consumed with sensual and evil thoughts.

d. Thoughts, impressions, or feelings that can be demonically inspired.

5. **_The Reprobate mind_** (defined as)

The mind that knowingly refuses truth and allows deception by evil and self-serving desires.

> 2 Thessalonians 2:10-12 (NLT) *He will use every kind of evil deception to fool those on their way to destruction, because they refuse to love and accept the truth that would save them. 11 So God will cause them to be greatly deceived, and they will believe these lies. 12 Then they will be condemned for enjoying evil rather than believing the truth.*

> 1 Timothy 4:2 (NLT) *These people are hypocrites and liars, and their consciences are dead.*

SESSION 3: Ministering the Mind of Christ

Key Points:

a. The reprobate mind has a seared conscience. The reprobate mind has forsaken and rejected God, being so hardened as to feel no remorse.

b. God confirms the person's delusion and allows their hearts to be so hardened and the more you rebel against God and separate yourself from Him, the harder it is to return back to him.

c. The person with a reprobate mind is turned over to self-delusion and demonic obsession.

II. THE MIND IS LIKE THE SOIL OF THE EARTH

- **The "Parable of the Sower" suggests four minds as four types of ground.**

    Luke 8:11-15 (NLT) *This is the meaning of the parable: The seed is God's word.* **12** *The seeds that fell on the footpath represent those who hear the message, only to have the devil come and take it away from their hearts and prevent them from believing and being saved.* **13** *The seeds on the rocky soil represent those who hear the message and receive it with joy. But since they don't have deep roots, they believe for a while, then they fall away when they face temptation.* **14** *The seeds that fell among the thorns represent those who hear the message, but all too quickly the message is crowded out by the cares and riches and pleasures of this life. And so they never grow into maturity.* **15** *And the seeds that fell on the good soil represent honest,* *good-hearted people who hear God's word, cling to it, and patiently produce a huge harvest.*

A. Cultivated ground/cultivated mind & heart

1. It's always a heart thing with God. A part of our emotions He strongly examines.

2. The human mind can be likened to a farmer's field.

3. As we allow the Holy Spirit to reveal and deal with our attitudes, mindsets, and thought processes, we produce a mind cultivated by the power of the Word of God and the heart of God.

4. We are continually weeding the garden of our minds and will ultimately put on the mind of Christ described in Romans 12:2 (NLT) *Don't copy the behavior and customs of this world, but let God transform you into a new person by changing the way you think. Then you will learn to know God's will for you, which is good and pleasing and perfect.*

   John 7:38 (NKJV) *"He who believes in Me, as the Scripture has said, out of his heart will flow rivers of living water."*

   Luke 8:11-15 (NLT) *This is the meaning of the parable: The seed is God's word.* 12 *The seeds that fell on the footpath represent those who hear the message, only to have the devil come and take it away from their hearts and prevent them from believing and being saved.* 13 *The seeds on the rocky soil represent those who hear the message and receive it with joy. But since they don't have deep*

SESSION 3: Ministering the Mind of Christ

roots, they believe for a while, then they fall away when they face temptation. **14** *The seeds that fell among the thorns represent those who hear the message, but all too quickly the message is crowded out by the cares and riches and pleasures of this life. And so they never grow into maturity.* **15** *And the seeds that fell on the good soil represent honest, good-hearted people who hear God's word, cling to it, and patiently produce a huge harvest.*

B. The Sower is Jesus/The Soil is the heart or mind of a person/and the seed is the Word of God

1. **Foot Path**: Some who hear the message only to have the devil come and steal away from their hearts, allowing their hearts to harden, who actually hear the word but don't accept it.

2. **Stoney Ground** - Rocky Soil: Is someone that shows interest in or has an awareness of the gospel, yet their heart isn't fully convicted so that when troubles come their faith isn't strong enough to stand. So, they fall away into temptation.

3. **Thorny Ground** – Thorny Patch: Is someone who received the gospel, but who has many other idols and distractions in life. Samples of this are materialism, lust, and worries, which take over their minds and hearts and won't allow room for Jesus to grow in His words with strong convictions or maturity.

4. **Good Soil**: Someone who has heard the gospel of the Word, received the Word of God and allowed it to take root within their life from the Holy Spirit. Jesus taught the parable Sower and Jesus is the sower, the soil is the heart or mind of the person, and the seed is the Word of God.

Through prayer, praise and worship, we recognize and invite God's presence, power, and anointing. The well water from God's reservoirs and underground rivers, which is the river of life flowing from the heart of those who believe, John 7:38 (NKJV) *"He who believes in Me, as the Scripture has said, out of his heart will flow rivers of living water."*

Jesus referred to the living water to indicate eternal life. He used the term to refer to the Holy Spirit. The two go together. The Holy Spirit is excepted, he brings eternal life. Jesus referred to the term, "come and drink," in promising the Holy Spirit to all who believed in Him, as an invitation, to come and accept His deeply satisfying love and also receive the empowerment from Holy Spirit.

SESSION 4: The Revelation Gifts

Key Verse: 1 Corinthians 14:39-40 (NKJV)
39 Therefore, brethren, desire earnestly to prophesy, and do not forbid to speak with tongues. 40 Let all things be done decently and in order.

The Purpose: To define and give examples of the category of giftings we call "revelation gifts." The believer will be able to identify them, understand how each operates and discuss their major purposes in the Church.

I. WORD OF KNOWLEDGE

Matthew 13:17 (NLT) *I tell you the truth, many prophets and righteous people longed to see what you see, but they didn't see it. And they longed to hear what you hear, but they didn't hear it.*

Words of knowledge can reveal someone's past that God wants them to release. Or it can reveal something in the present. It will always reveal something hidden from human knowledge. This gift can also bring about a solution.

A. Word of knowledge (defined as);

1. A supernatural revelation by the Holy Spirit of specific facts.

2. Instant knowledge.

SESSION 4: The Revelation Gifts

3. God's knowledge is imparted as a word to a believer to reveal the hidden facts of a circumstance or a matter. It also can reveal something about a person's past that God wants them to release or regarding the present time.

4. From God's infinite knowledge.

5. A word for a particular season, time, person (or people), for a purpose, or a need at a particular place.

The gifting is NOT:

- knowledge as an amplification of human knowledge.
- knowledge by intellectual capability.
- knowledge based on study.
- knowledge acquired through earning it; It is a gift by faith.

B. Two levels of knowledge

1. Human or natural knowledge/which is naturally obtained, coming from you as a person.

2. The Word of Knowledge/Holy Spirit Gifting is the operation of the gifts of the Holy Spirit wherein an individual receives a thought from the heart of God and expresses an inspired word by faith for the growth and establishment of His Church. It is beyond the natural; it is of God's higher thoughts and ways.

C. Biblical examples of word of knowledge

> 1 Samuel 9:15-16 (NLT) *Now the Lord had told Samuel the previous day,* **16** *"About this time tomorrow I will send you a man from the land of Benjamin. Anoint him to*

SPIRITUAL GIFTS

be the leader of my people, Israel. He will rescue them from the Philistines, for I have looked down on my people in mercy and have heard their cry."

1. The word of knowledge has the ability to penetrate through all human facades and pretenses. A perfect example of this is found in 1 Kings 14:1-5 (NLT):

   At that time Jeroboam's son Abijah became very sick. 2 So Jeroboam told his wife, "Disguise yourself so that no one will recognize you as my wife. Then go the prophet Ahijah at Shiloh – the man who told me I would become king. 3 Take him a gift of ten loaves of bread, some cakes, and a jar of honey, and ask him, what will happen to the boy." 4 So Jeroboam's wife went to Ahijah's home at Shiloh, He was an old man now and could no longer see. 5 But the Lord had told Ahijah, Jeroboam's wife will come here, pretending to be someone else. She will ask you about her son, for he is very sick. Give her the answer I give you."

Caution when it comes to greed. Greed was revealed to the prophet as a word of knowledge.

   2 Kings 5:20-27 (NLT) 20 But Gehazi, the servant of Elisha, the man of God, said to himself, "My master should not have let this Aramean get away without accepting any of his gifts. As surely as the Lord lives, I will chase after him and get something from him." 21 So Gehazi set off after Naaman. When Naaman saw Gehazi running after him, he climbed down from his chariot and went to meet him. "Is everything all right?" Naaman asked?" 22 "Yes, Gehazi said, "but my master has sent me to tell you that two young prophets from the hill country of Ephraim have just

SESSION 4: The Revelation Gifts

> *arrived. He would like 75 pounds of silver and two sets of clothing to give to them." 23 "By all means, take twice as much silver", Naaman insisted. He gave him two sets of clothing and tied up the money in two bags, and sent two of his servants to carry the gifts for Gehazi. 24 But when they arrived at the citadel, Gehazi took the gifts from the servants and sent the men back. Then he went and hid the gifts inside the house. 25 When he went in to his master, Elisha asked him, "Where have you been, Gehazi?" "I haven't been anywhere", he replied. 26 But Elisha asked him, "Don't you realize that I was there in spirit when Naaman stepped down from his chariot to meet you? Is this the time to receive money and clothing, olive groves and vineyards, sheep and cattle, and male and female servants? 27 Because you have done this, you and your descendants will suffer from Naaman's leprosy forever." When Gehazi left the room, he was covered with leprosy; his skin was as white as snow.*

2. Jesus met a Samaritan woman. This is an example of evangelism with a word of knowledge. God wants all saints to move in all nine gifts. John 4:18, 19, 29 (NLT) *18 "for you have had five husbands, and you aren't even married to the man you're living with now. You certainly spoke the truth!" 19 "Sir," the woman said, "you must be a prophet."... 29 "come and see a man who told me everything I ever did! Could he possibly be the Messiah?"*

3. Jesus received a word of knowledge about Nathanael in John 1:47-49 (NLT) *47As they approached, Jesus said, "Now here is a genuine son of Israel – a man of complete integrity." 48 How do you know about me?" Nathanael asked. Jesus replied, "I could see you under the fig tree before Philip found you." 49 Then Nathanael exclaimed, Rabbi, you are the Son of God – the King of Israel!"*

4. The word of knowledge delivered in due season goes straight to the heart and opens the door for God to minister.

D. How does the word of knowledge operate?

1. Motivated by the Spirit.

2. Activated by the faith of the individual.

3. Ministered in obedience to the Word of God.

4. Developed by reason of use.

E. Some purposes of the word of knowledge

1. To reveal the cause of sickness or demonic possession.

2. To reveal root problems.

3. To reveal secrets of men's hearts so that repentance comes.

4. To give insight into people's lives for intercessory prayer.

II. WORD OF WISDOM

1 Corinthians 14:12 (NLT) And the same is true for you. Since you are so eager to have the special abilities the Spirit gives, seek those that will strengthen the whole church.

We ought to be zealous for the gifts the Spirit of God chooses to release, God's manifold wisdom about future circumstances, the cause of a situation, or the answer to a problem.

A. Word of wisdom (biblically defined as)

The supernatural ability in the Spirit to impart special and specific insight, instruction, guidance or counsel. It brings life-changing

SESSION 4: The Revelation Gifts

illumination and aids in making course-changing decisions. A word of wisdom is a capacity of the mind that allows us to understand life from God's perspective.

Key Point: Another way to describe wisdom is the moral skill for living revealed through God's word.

James 3:17 (NLT) *But the wisdom from above is first of all pure. It is also peace-loving, gentle at all times, and willing to yield to others. It is full of mercy and the fruit of good deeds. It shows no favoritism and is always sincere.*

Human wisdom is not God's wisdom, covering up the truth with the unholy heart condition of jealousy and selfishness, ungodly boasting with lying. Human wisdom is flawed, and self-seeking, leading to destruction.

1. God's practical wisdom relates to our lives even during the most trying times. It is not isolated from suffering and trials but gives resolutions to overcome them. An intelligent person may have profound ideas, but a wise person puts profound ideas into ACTION for the best outcome.

2. God's wisdom is divine. God's wisdom goes beyond common sense. Common sense does not help to react joyfully in the midst of adversity. His wisdom begins with respect for Him and leads us to follow His direction and increase our ability to tell right from wrong, as related in James 3:17 (referenced above).

3. God's wisdom is Christlike. When we ask for God's wisdom we are ultimately asking to be more like Christ with the wisdom of God.

> ***a.** 1 Corinthians 1:24 (NLT) But to those called by God to salvation, both Jews and Gentiles, Christ is the power of God and the wisdom of God.*
>
> ***b.** 1 Corinthians 2:1-7 (NLT) When I first came to you, dear brothers and sisters, I didn't use lofty words and impressive wisdom to tell you God's secret plan. 2 For I decided that while I was with you I would forget everything except Jesus Christ, the one who was crucified. 3 I came to you in weakness – timid and trembling. 4 And my message and my preaching were very plain. Rather than using clever and persuasive speeches, I relied only on the power of the Holy Spirit. 5 I did this so you would trust not in human wisdom but in the power of God. 6 Yet when I am among mature believers, I do speak with words of wisdom, but not the kind of wisdom that belongs to this world or to the rulers of this world, who are soon forgotten. 7 No the wisdom we speak of is the mystery of God – his plan that was previously hidden, even though he made it for our ultimate glory before the world began.*

4. Holy Spirit Gift of the Word of Wisdom:

   a. God-given wisdom and revelation for the purposes of God concerning people, things, or events presently or in the future.

   b. The word of wisdom tells us how to apply the recently revealed facts or knowledge.

   c. The heart of God giving strategy, insight, or plans not yet revealed.

   It is **NOT**:

SESSION 4: The Revelation Gifts

    a. Revelation of the written Word.

    b. Anything that contradicts the written Word of God.

    c. Human reasoning.

An individual can move in all the gifts of the Spirit and not have mature Christian wisdom. Maturity is Christian character, integrity and meekness before God. The gifts operate by faith.

B. Biblical examples of the word of wisdom

Read the following Scriptures:

Genesis chapter 41, Exodus chapter 3, and *Genesis chapter 19.*

In Genesis chapter 41 we see Joseph interpreted Pharoah's dreams by receiving revelation from God in order to perceive the true interpretation. By a word of wisdom, Joseph warned Pharoah of the seven-year famine.

C. How does the word of wisdom operate?

1 Corinthians 2:6-7 (NLT) *Yet when I am among mature believers, I do speak with words of wisdom, but not the kind of wisdom that belongs to this world or to the rulers of this world, who are soon forgotten. 7 No the wisdom we speak of is the mystery of God – his plan that was previously hidden, even though he made it for our ultimate glory before the world began.*

    1. Motivated by the Holy Spirit.

    2. Activated by faith.

    3. Can be a flash of revelation or special insight in thoughts, vision, slight mental impression, or prophetic flow.

SPIRITUAL GIFTS

    4. Is only learned by exercising the gift.

D. Some of the purposes of word of wisdom

1. To warn of impending danger. Matthew 24:4-6 (NLT) *Jesus told them, "Don't let anyone mislead you, 5 for many will come in my name claiming, 'I am the Messiah.' They will deceive many. 6 And you will hear of wars and threats of wars, but don't panic. Yes, these things must take place, but the end won't follow immediately."*

2. To make known or confirm a ministry call. Ephesians 4:12 (NLT) Their responsibility is to equip God's people to do his work and build up the church, the body of Christ.

3. To give instruction on how things are to be done God's way, as well as providing solutions. Matthew 24:30 (NLT) And then at last, the sign that the Son of Man is coming will appear in the heavens, and there will be deep mourning among all peoples of the earth. And they will see the Son of Man coming on the clouds of heaven with power and great glory.

4. To give insight and understanding that will advance His cause, in others and you. Isaiah 9:6-7 (NLT) For a child is born to us, a son is given to us. The government will rest on his shoulders. And he will be called: Wonderful Counselor, Mighty God, Everlasting Father, Prince of Peace. 7 His government and its peace will never end. He will rule with fairness and justice from the throne of his ancestor David for all eternity. The passionate commitment of the Lord of Heaven's Armies will make this happen!

Marketplace ministry will be the new frontier for Kingdom advancement in the Saints Movement.

SESSION 4: The Revelation Gifts

III. DISCERNING OF SPIRITS

> Acts 16:16-19 (NLT) *One day as we were going down to the place of prayer, we met a slave girl who had a spirit that enabled her to tell the future. She earned a lot of money for her masters by telling fortunes.* **17** *She followed Paul and the rest of us, shouting, "These men are servants of the Most High God, and they have come to tell you how to be saved."* **18** *This went on day after day until Paul got so exasperated that he turned and said to the demon within her, "I command you in the name of Jesus Christ to come out of her." And instantly it left her.* **19** *Her masters' hopes of wealth were now shattered, so they grabbed Paul and Silas and dragged them before the authorities at the marketplace.*

Discerning of spirits releases insight into the spiritual world, revelation of angelic visitation, discerning of devils, and unclean spirits. You walk into an atmosphere and feel uneasy or the presence of oppressing spirits. Remember to deal with the spirit and not the person. This is not a fault-finding gift.

A. **DISCERNING OF SPIRITS** (defined as)

The supernatural ability to discern which spirit is motivating human words and behaviors. It is a quickening sense in the spirit by the Spirit into the realm of the spirit or the spiritual world. There are three sources of spirits: *human, satanic,* and *Godly.*

SPIRITUAL GIFTS

> 1 Corinthians 12:3 (NLT) *So I want you to know that no one speaking by the Spirit of God will curse Jesus, and no one can say Jesus is Lord, except by the Holy Spirit.*

> 1 John 4:1 (NLT) *Dear friends, do not believe everyone who claims to speak by the Spirit. You must test them to see if the spirit they have comes from God. For there are many false prophets in the world.*

The two examples above touch first on the Spirit of God and then on evil or demonic spirits. Other than these two there is the human spirit. The human spirit has natural characteristics which include, intellect, emotions, fears, passions, and creativity. In the absence of being of the Holy Spirit or of an evil or demonic spirit, these characteristics are merely and simply motivated by and reveal a human spirit.

The discerning of spirits operates on two levels, general and specific.

1. <u>General</u>: The determination of the "spiritual source" of a word, attitude, or individual action, an atmosphere or environment corporately helping to determine if something is of human origin, divine or devilish.

    The Bible refers to the word of God,
    > 1 Peter 1:23-25 (NLT) *For you have been born again, but not to a life that will quickly end. Your new life will last forever because it comes from the eternal, living word of God. 24 As the Scriptures say, "People are like grass; their beauty is like a flower in the field. The grass withers and the flower fades. 25 But the word of*

SESSION 4: The Revelation Gifts

the Lord remains forever. And that word is the Good News that was preached to you.

The Bible refers to the doctrine and traditions of men,
Colossians 2:22 (NLT) *Such rules are mere human teachings about things that deteriorate as we use them.*

The Bible refers to the doctrine of demons,
1 Timothy 4:1 (NLT) *Now the Holy Spirit tells us clearly that in the last times some will turn away from the true faith; they will follow deceptive spirits and teachings that come from demons.*

1 Corinthians 1:30 (NLT) *Just as there is the wisdom of God, God has united you with Christ Jesus. For our benefit God made him to be wisdom itself. Christ made us right with God; he made us pure and holy, and he freed us from sin.*

There is the wisdom of man,
1 Corinthians 1:20 (NLT) *So where does this leave the philosophers, the scholars, and the world's brilliant debaters?*

1 Corinthians 2:4-5 (NLT) *And my message and my preaching were very plain. Rather than using clever and persuasive speeches, I relied only on the power of the Holy Spirit. 5 I did this so you would trust not in human wisdom but in the power of God.*

SPIRITUAL GIFTS

And there is the counsel of the ungodly,

> Psalm 1:1 (NLT) *Oh, the joys of those who do not follow the advice of the wicked, or stand around with sinners, or join in with mockers.*

> James 3:15 (NLT) *For jealousy and selfishness are not God's kind of wisdom. Such things are earthly, unspiritual, and demonic.*

2. <u>Specific</u>: The ability to identify specific evil spirits and their devices. Discerning of spirits is a safeguard against deception. (Read Acts 13:6-12 (NKJV), specifically verses 9-11:

> Acts 13:9-11 (NKJV), *Then Saul, who also is called Paul, filled with the Holy Spirit, looked intently at him 10 and said, "O full of all deceit and all fraud, you son of the devil, you enemy of all righteousness, will you not cease perverting the straight ways of the Lord? 11 And now, indeed, the hand of the Lord is upon you, and you shall be blind, not seeing the sun for a time." And immediately a dark mist fell on him, and he went around seeking someone to lead him by the hand.*

The gift is not a keen human insight or an evaluation based on what is seen. These chapters and verses give us better examples of this world we cannot see.

> Acts 16:16-18 (NKJV) *Now it happened, as we went to prayer, that a certain slave girl possessed with a spirit of divination met us, who brought her masters much profit by fortune-telling. 17 This girl followed Paul and us, and*

SESSION 4: The Revelation Gifts

cried out, saying, "These men are the servants of the Most High God, who proclaim to us the way of salvation." *18 And this she did for many days. But Paul, greatly [a]annoyed, turned and said to the spirit, "I command you in the name of Jesus Christ to come out of her." And he came out that very hour.*

B. THREE LEVELS OF DISCERNING

1. <u>Natural</u>: Perception through observing actions, words, and mannerisms.

2. <u>Psychic</u>: Is not of God. A "gate of hell" is opened by psychic activity. Some people have a gift of spiritual heightened gifting but don't walk with God. They misunderstand and misapply that spiritual consciousness, opening themselves to dark spiritual forces. Without discerning the spirits these people call themselves psychics.

3. <u>Divine Gift</u>: The God-given gift to see with spiritual eyes what the Holy Spirit reveals to us within each of the three spiritual realms, that of the first, second, and third heaven. And to discern by the use of the gift whether the motive or origin of a word, action, attitude, or atmosphere is of the Holy Spirit or any other spirit. To discern whether it is from our human spirit, from God, or a demonic spirit. When from a demonic spirit the discerning of spirits allows you to not only see that it is demonic but also to discern the demonic spirit in operation.

Colossians 1:13 (NLT) *For he has rescued us from the kingdom of darkness and transferred us into the Kingdom of his dear Son.*

Genesis 28:12 (NLT) *As he slept, he dreamed of a stairway that reached from the earth up to heaven. And he saw the angels of God going up and down the stairway.*

Deuteronomy 10:14 *"Look, the highest heavens and the earth and everything in it all belong to the Lord your God."*

Psalm 19:1 (NLT) *The heavens proclaim the glory of God. The skies display his craftsmanship.*

We speak of three heavens. The first is the atmosphere that surrounds the earth. It is the air we breathe and the sky where birds fly and clouds form. The second heaven is beyond the first heaven. It is where the sun, moon, stars, and other celestial bodies are located. The third heaven is the dwelling place of God. The throne room of God is in the third heaven. While spirits do move and have an effect on the natural things which do exist in the first and second heaven, the third heaven is a strictly spiritual realm. It is where Jesus sits at the right hand of the Father.

- **Three Heavenly Realms:**

    1. <u>Atmospheric Realm</u> (first heavenly realm) – where humans and creatures live on earth, where birds fly, and where Satan dwells as prince of the power of the air. (Genesis 1:14-15, 17, 20), (Daniel 2:37-38), (Psalms 104:12)

SESSION 4: The Revelation Gifts

2. <u>Celestial Realm</u> (second heavenly realm) – where angels fly and do battle. Also, where Satan and his fallen angels who were forced out of heaven, having lost their battle against Michael and his angels (when we encounter them on earth they are often referred to as demons), are battling even now. (Revelations 12:4-12, 14:6,7)

3. <u>Throne Room of God</u> (Third heavenly realm) – where God dwells.

> *II Corinthians 12:2-4 (NLT) I was caught up to the third heaven fourteen years ago. Whether I was in my body or out of my body, I don't know – only God knows. 3 Yes, only God knows whether I was in my body or outside my body. But I do know 4 that I was caught up to paradise and heard these things so astounding that they cannot be expressed in words, things no human is allowed to tell.*

While spirits do move and have an effect on the natural things which do exist in the first and second heavenly realms, the third heaven is **restricted only to God** where Jesus sits at the right hand of the Father.

C. BIBLICAL EXAMPLES

1. In Matthew 16:21-23, Jesus discerned that Peter was speaking from the wrong spirit and said, "Get thee behind me Satan."
2. In Acts 8:23, Peter discerned that Simon's motives were wrong when he asked for the Holy Spirit.
3. In Acts 16:16-18, Paul discerned a woman at Philippi was possessed with a spirit of divination.

Matthew 16:21-23 (NLT) *From then on Jesus began to tell his disciples plainly that it was necessary for him to go to Jerusalem, and that he would suffer many terrible things at the hands of the elders, the leading priests, and the teachers of religious law. He would be killed, but on the third day he would be raised form the dead.* **22** *But Peter took him aside and began to reprimand him for saying such things. "Heaven forbid, Lord," he said. "This will never happen to you!"* **23** *Jesus turned to Peter and said, "Get away from me, Satan! You are a dangerous trap to me. You are seeing things merely from a human point of view, not from God's."*

Acts 8:21-23 (NLT) *You have no part in this, for your heart is not right with God.* **22** *Repent of your wickedness and pray to the Lord. Perhaps he will forgive your evil thoughts,* **23** *for I can see that you are full of bitter jealousy and are held captive by sin."*

Acts 16:16-18 (NLT) *One day as we were going down to the place of prayer, we met a slave girl who had a spirit that enabled her to tell the future. She earning a lot of money for her masters by telling fortunes.* **17** *She followed Paul and the rest of us, shouting, "There men are servants of the Most High God, and they have come to tell you how to be saved."* **18** *This went on day after day until Paul got so exasperated that he turned and said to the demon within her, "I command you in the name of Jesus Christ to come out of her." And instantly it left her.*

SESSION 4: The Revelation Gifts

D. HOW DOES THE GIFT OF DISCERNING OF SPIRITS OPERATE?

The Holy Spirit gives you insight into the spirit realm. You have "Angelic-like" revelation from God by the Holy Spirit, as He wills.

1. It is motivated by the Holy Spirit and activated by the individual's faith. You can feel and sense things from Heaven. Exodus 33:18-23 (NLT) Moses responded, *18 "Then show me your glorious presence." 19 The Lord replied, "I will make all my goodness pass before you, and I will call out my name, Yahweh, before you. For I will show mercy to anyone I choose, and I will show compassion to anyone I choose. 20 But you may not look directly at my face, for no one may see me and live." 21 The Lord continued, "Look, stand near me on this rock. 22 I will hide you in the crevice of the rock and cover you with my hand until I have passed by. 23 Then I will remove my hand and let you see me from behind. But my face will not be seen."*

2. It can come as a flash of revelation in your thoughts, a vision, or through prophetic flow. It includes the discerning activity going on in the spirit realm.

3. It can come as an inner alert as the spirit realm affects our physical senses. Hebrews 5:14 says we have our senses exercised to know (discern) both good and evil. You can just sense things that are unsettling to your spirit. Or sense a feeling of oppressiveness.

CAUTION: Never attribute critical or judgmental thinking to this gifting. The Lord does not sanction fault-finding or flesh detectives operating out of divisive and unloving hearts.

We must train our consciences, our senses, our minds, and our bodies to be able to distinguish good from evil. For example, can you discern Holy Spirit-led teaching versus a false teacher?

E. SOME OF THE PURPOSES OF THE GIFT OF DISCERNING OF SPIRITS:

1. To reveal demonic principalities and powers over geographical areas.

2. To reveal specific demonic spirits that are hindering or possessing people.

3. To reveal what is in an individual's human spirit that would cause them to say or act in a particular manner.

4. To reveal the direction and flow that the Holy Spirit has for a service.

Ephesians 6:10-12 (NLT) *A final word: Be strong in the Lord and in his mighty power. 11 Put on all of God's armor so that you will be able to stand firm against all strategies of the devil. 12 For we are not fighting against flesh-and-blood enemies, but against evil rulers and authorities of the unseen world, against mighty powers in this dark world, and against evil spirits in the heavenly places.*

Acts 16:16-19 (NLT) *One day as we were going down to the place of prayer, we met a slave girl who had a spirit that enabled her to tell the future. She earned a lot of money for her masters by telling fortunes. 17 She followed Paul and the rest of us, shouting, "There men are servants of the Most High God, and they have come to tell you how to be saved."*

SESSION 4: The Revelation Gifts

***18** This went on day after day until Paul got so exasperated that he turned and said to the demon within her, "I command you in the name of Jesus Christ to come out of her." And instantly it left her. **19** Her masters' hopes of wealth were now shattered, so they grabbed Paul and Silas and dragged them before the authorities at the marketplace.*

F. FINAL NOTES ON THE DISCERNING OF SPIRITS

When operating in the discerning of spirits we are involving ourselves in the heavenly realms, and we discern the kingdom of darkness.

The Greek word for heaven is "epouranios" meaning sphere of spiritual activities. Heavenly realm can refer to both angelic and demonic activities. As in Ephesians 1:19-20 and Ezekiel 28:11-17 we can't see, hear, or touch it. The Bible assumes it. We can glean insight into a world we cannot see, by studying what God tells us about it. God is spirit, as we are told in John 4:24. Heavens refer to the atmosphere, Genesis 1:1 and Psalm 148:4, and the Heavenly realm which encompasses all spirit beings. We will spend most of our lives in the Heavenly Realms, 2 Corinthians 5:1 and John 5:11.

> Ephesians 1:19-20 (NLT) *I also pray that you will understand the incredible greatness of God's power for us who believe him. This is the same mighty power **20** that raised Christ from the dead and seated him in the place of honor at God's right hand in the heavenly realms.*

> Ezekiel 28:11-17 (NLT) *Then this further message came to me from the Lord: **12** "Son of man, sing this funeral song for the king of Tyre. Give him this message from the Sovereign*

Lord: *13 "You were the model of perfection, full of wisdom and exquisite in beauty. You were in Eden, the garden of God. Your clothing was adorned with every precious stone – red carnelian, pale-green peridot, white moonstone, blue-green beryl, onyx, green jasper, blue lapis, lazuli, turquoise, and emerald – all beautifully crafted for you and set in the finest gold. They were given to you on the day you were created. 14 I ordained and anointed you as the mighty angelic guardian. You had access to the holy mountain of God and walked among the stones of fire. 15 "You were blameless in all you did from the day you were created until the day evil was found in you. 16 Your rich commerce led you to violence, and you sinned. So I banished you in disgrace from the mountain of God. I expelled you, O mighty guardian, from your place among the stones of fire. 17 Your heart was filled with pride because of all your beauty. Your wisdom was corrupted by your love of splendor. So I threw you to the ground and exposed you to the curious gaze of kings.*

John 4:24 (NLT) *"For God is Spirit, so those who worship him must worship in spirit and in truth."*

Genesis 1:1 (NLT) *In the beginning God created the heavens and the earth.*

Psalm 148:4 *Praise him, sun and moon! Praise him, all you twinkling stars!*

2 Corinthians 5:1 (NLT) *For we know that when this earthly tent we live in is taken down (that is, when we die and leave*

SESSION 4: The Revelation Gifts

this earthly body), we will have a house in heaven, an eternal body made for us by God himself and not by human hands.

John 5:11 (NLT) *But he replied, "The man who healed me told me, 'Pick up your mat and walk.'"*

God's home is Heaven. This is not to be confused with heavenly realms. Heaven is a heavenly realm, but it is more than just that. It is the very home of God and the place of His eternal throne. God exists outside of the bounds of time, space, and matter.

Acts 7:55-56 (NLT) *But Stephen, full of the Holy Spirit, gazed steadily into heaven and saw the glory of God, and he saw Jesus standing in the place of honor at God's right hand. 56 And he told them, "Look, I see the heavens opened and the Son of Man standing in the place of honor at God's right hand!"*

The kingdom of darkness is very real. Daniel chapter 10 gives us a very powerful picture of just how real it is.

Daniel 10:12-14 *Then he said, "Don't be afraid, Daniel. Since the first day you began to pray for understanding and to humble yourself before your God, your request has been heard in heaven. I have come in answer to your prayer. 13 But for twenty-one days the spirit prince of the kingdom of Persia blocked my way. Then Michael, one of the archangels, came to help me, and I left him there with the spirit prince of the kingdom of Persia. 14 Now I am here to explain what will happen to your people in the future, for this vision concerns a time yet to come."*

The kingdom of darkness, Satanic dark side of heavenly realms seems to belong to Satan and his evil spirits at this time. Satan is not a counterpart to God. God has no challengers at all. The only power that Satan has is allowed by God.

Isaiah 14:12 (NLT) *"How you are fallen from heaven, O shining star, son of the morning! You have been thrown down to the earth, you who destroyed the nations of the world."*

Luke 22:31-32 (NLT) *"Simon, Simon, Satan has asked to sift each of you like wheat. 32 But I have pleaded in prayer for you, Simon, that your faith should not fail. So when you have repented and turned to me again, strengthen your brothers."*

Revelation 12:12 (NLT) *"Therefore rejoice, O heavens! And you who live in the heavens, rejoice! But terror will come on the earth and the sea, for the devil has come down to you in great anger, knowing that he has little time."*

Session 5: THE INSPIRATIONAL GIFTS

Key Verse: 1 Corinthians 14:22-25 (NLT)
22 So you see that speaking in tongues is a sign, not for believers, but for unbelievers. Prophecy, however, is for the benefit of believers, not unbelievers. 23 Even so, if unbelievers or people who don't understand these things come into your church meeting and hear everyone speaking in an unknown language, they will think you are crazy. 24 But if all of you are prophesying, and unbelievers or people who don't understand such things come into your meeting, they will be convicted or sin and judged by what you say. 25 As they listen, their secret thoughts will be exposed, and they will fall to their knees and worship God, declaring, "God is truly among you."

The Purpose: To define and give examples of the category of giftings we call "inspirational gifts." The believer will be able to identify them, understand how each operates and discuss their major purposes in the Church.

I. THE GIFT OF DIFFERENT KINDS OF TONGUES

Acts 2:4-11 (NLT) *And everyone present was filled with the Holy Spirit and began speaking in other languages, as the Holy Spirit gave them this ability. 5 At that time there were devout Jews from every nation living in Jerusalem. 6 When they heard the loud noise, everyone came running, and they were bewildered to hear their own languages being spoken by the believers. 7 They were completely amazed. "How can this be?"*

they exclaimed. "These people are all from Galilee, 8 and yet we hear them speaking in own native languages!"

Speaking in tongues is a powerful demonstration of the Holy Spirit in operation and is a supernatural utterance unknown to man but known to God. The closer we draw to God Himself, the more we inherit an understanding of this as His own language because He speaks all of them. Through this very special gift of His, we get to partake in such a beautiful connection with Him and through the Holy Spirit, as He yields understanding of this gift in operation.

II. THE GIFT OF INTERPRETATION OF TONGUES

1 Corinthians 14:10-13 (NLT) There are many different languages in the world, and every language has meaning. 11 But if I don't understand a language, I will be a foreigner to someone who speaks it, and the one who speaks it will be a foreigner to me. 12 And the same is true for you. Since you are so eager to have the special abilities the Spirit gives, seek those that will strengthen the whole church. 13 So anyone who speaks in tongues should pray also for the ability to interpret what has been said.

If a person has the gift of interpretation of tongues, then tongues can be used in public worship. If speaking in tongues in public the one speaking is praying that one is present who receives the interpretation, or they should pray for the interpretation. That way the entire church will be edified.

III. THE GIFT OF PROPHECY

> 1 Corinthians 14:1-4 (NLT) *Let love be your highest goal! But you should also desire the special abilities the Spirit gives – especially the ability to prophesy. 2 For if you have the ability to speak in tongues, you will be talking only to God, since people won't be able to understand you. You will be speaking by the power of the Spirit, but it will all be mysterious. 3 But one who prophesies strengthens others, encourages them, and comforts them. 4 A person who speaks in tongues is strengthened personally, but one who speaks a word of prophecy strengthens the entire church.*

The ability to prophesy may involve future events but its main purpose is to communicate God's messages to people providing insight, warning, correction, and encouragement. It is the intimacy of sharing God's love in communion with Him, drawing people closer, to hear His voice and grasp His heart and mind. In my experience, loving the giver more than the gift is a key to prophecies that are confirmed in those who receive them, drawing people more importantly to Him and hearing His voice.

SESSION 5: The Inspirational Gifts

SPIRITUAL GIFTS

Session 6: THE POWER GIFTS

Key Verse: John 14:12-14 (NLT)
12 "I tell you the truth, anyone who believes in me will do the same works I have done, and ever greater works, because I am going to be with the Father. 13 You can ask for anything in my name, and I will do it, so that the Son can bring glory to the Father. 14 Yes, ask me for anything in my name, and I will do it!

The Purpose: To learn that Power is the ability to act or to produce an effect, to exercise authority or influence over others. This power comes only from God and is exercised through our weakness and not by our own strength. It is all the Holy Spirit and not us. The reason we refer to these as the Power Gifts is each one of these gifts does something or accomplishes something for the Kingdom of God.

A. THE GIFT OF WORKING OF MIRACLES

John 5:19-21 (NLT) *So Jesus explained, "I tell you the truth, the Son can do nothing by himself. He does only what he sees the Father doing. Whatever the Father does, the Son also does. 20 For the Father loves the Son and shows him everything he is doing. In fact, the Father will show him how to do even greater works than healing this man. Then you will truly be astonished. 21 For just as the Father gives life to those he raises from the dead, so the Son gives life to anyone he wants.*

SESSION 6: The Power Gifts

The working of miracles is an extraordinary and astonishing happening that is attributed to the presence and action of an ultimate and divine power, that is God Himself. Because of the perfect unity of Jesus Christ with the Father and Holy Spirit, this empowers the believer with confidence, insight, ability, boldness, and courage. Our identification is with Jesus, we must honor Him as He wants us to live, and we must make the right choices. When you see the working of miracles it gives you an encounter with God and His unlimited power, and that supernatural power can't be explained by natural law or human ability; these are the works inspired by the Heavenly Father.

> Acts 1:6-8 (NLT) *So when the apostles were with Jesus, they kept asking him, "Lord, has the time come for you to free Israel and restore our kingdom?" 7 He replied, "The Father alone has the authority to set those dates and times, and they are not for you to know. 8 But you will receive power when the Holy Spirit comes upon you. And you will be my witnesses, telling people about me everywhere – in Jerusalem, throughout Judea, in Samaria, and to the ends of the earth."*

B. THE GIFT OF FAITH

> Ephesians 2:8-9 (NKJV) *For by grace you have been saved through faith, and that not of yourselves; it is the gift of God, 9 not of works, lest anyone should boast.*

> Hebrews 11:1, 3 (KJV) *Now faith is the substance of things hoped for, the evidence of things not seen…3 through faith we understand that the worlds were framed by the word of*

> *God, so that things which are seen were not made by things which do appear.*

The gift of faith enables one to demonstrate great confidence in the power and promises of God. No matter what circumstance might happen, nothing can shake their faith in God. Faith starts with believing in God, His goodness, and truth. That He is who He says He is. Faith culminates with knowing that God will do what He promises, just as Jesus demonstrated many times. A prime example is when He rebuked the wind. Mark 4:39 (NKJV) Then He arose and rebuked the wind, and said to the sea, "Peace, be still!" And the wind ceased and there was a great calm.

> Matthew 9:22 (NLT) *Jesus turned around, and when he saw her he said, "Daughter, be encouraged! Your faith has made you well!" And the woman was healed at that moment.*

C. THE GIFT OF HEALING

> Mark 16:17-18 (NKJV) *And these signs will follow those who believe: In My name they will cast out demons; they will speak with new tongues;* **18** *they will take up serpents; and if they drink anything deadly, it will by no means hurt them; they will lay hands on the sick, and they will recover."*

> Acts 3:6 (NKJV) *Then Peter said, "Silver and gold I do not have, but what I do have I give you: In the name of Jesus Christ of Nazareth, rise up and walk."*

SESSION 6: The Power Gifts

Supernatural elements are given to a believer to minister various kinds of healing and restoration to individuals through the power of the Holy Spirit. If you don't have compassion, it is impossible for the gift of healing to operate through you. If you don't desire to see the sick healed or if suffering people bother you, then you may not be used by the Holy Spirit with this gift. Not everyone has this desire.

Session 7: THE KEYS TO THE KINGDOM

Key Verse: Romans 12:6 (NLT)
6 In his grace, God has given us different gifts for doing certain things well. So if God has given you the ability to prophesy, speak out with as much faith as God has given you.

The Purpose: First and foremost, the purpose is to develop a greater intimacy with Christ. Part of the exciting adventure of following Christ involves discovering your spiritual gifts and more importantly, making them available to God and watching Him use them to accomplish more for His kingdom work than you ever thought possible. Making serving God and His people your primary motive as you utilize your gifts, especially in love. Let love be your highest goal.

> 1 Corinthians 13:1-3 (NLT) *If I could speak all the languages of earth and of angels, but didn't love others, I would only be a noisy gong or a clanging cymbal. 2 If I had the gift of prophecy, and if I understood all of God's secret plans and possessed all knowledge, and if I had such faith that I could move mountains, but didn't love others, I would be nothing. 3 If I gave everything I have to the poor and even sacrificed my body, I could boast about it; but if I didn't love others, I would have gained nothing.*

> 1 Corinthians 14:1 (NLT) *Let love be your highest goal! But you should also desire the special abilities the Spirit gives – especially the ability to prophesy.*

SESSION 7: The Keys to the Kingdom

1. **Keys are power and authority**, signifying a person and entrusting him or her with an important charge. Keys open doors (things), close doors, allow access into places, and lock doors, keeping out of places. While keys are transient, they can take you to a place God wants you to go. I say, "Many keys bring many Kingdom exploits".

    a. Isaiah 22:22 (NLT) *I will give him the key to the house of David – the highest position in the royal court. When he opens doors, no one will be able to close them; when he closes doors, no one will be able to open them.*

2. The **Key to the house of David** represented great authority for salvation (Isaiah 22:20-22 NKJV).

    Key Point: The keys of David is like the word of God in your mouth. You speak to a situation and circumstances based on your revelation of the word of God. You can shut down any unpleasant doors, and you can open the pleasant ones. The word of God can bring salvation to heal the sick, raise the dead, bring deliverance to the oppressed, and perform several signs and wonders. You rule with decrees like a king because you are in government reigning with Christ. You rule like Jesus on earth because you come from that lineage.

    a. Matthew 16:19 (NLT) *"And I will give you the keys of the kingdom of Heaven. Whatever you forbid on earth will be forbidden in heaven, and whatever you permit on earth will be permitted in heaven."*

    b. Revelation 3:7 (NLT) *"Write this letter to the angel of the church in Philadelphia. This is the message from the one who is holy and true, the one who has the key of David. What he opens no one can close; and what he closes, no one can open."*

3. Key of David, is Christ's authority to open doors into the future concerning salvation.

A. FIRST KEY – LOVE; God is Love.

Matthew 22:37-39 (NLT) *Jesus replied, "'You must love the Lord your God with all your heart, all your soul, and all your mind.' 38 This is the first and greatest commandment. 39 A second is equally important: 'Love your neighbor as yourself.'*

John 15:12-13 (NLT) *This is my commandment: Love each other in the same way I have loved you. 13 There is no greater love than to lay down one's life for one's friends.*

- **Sacrificial Love that we should put into use.**
    a. Listening to one another.
    b. Encouraging one another.
    c. Helping one another.
    d. Having a relationship with one another is vital.
    e. A heart of gratitude concerning one another.
    f. Not just being a "church buddy", but a friend in all aspects of friendship.
    g. Being intentional and sincere in relationship to one another.

SESSION 7: The Keys to the Kingdom

KEY POINT: First and foremost, obey God because you love Him, not by works or deeds, but because you know Him, and you know who He is. Put this in motion, making this your life purpose, and I guarantee you, that you will not fall short of loving others and effectively operating in this gift of the Spirit.

> 1 Corinthians 13:4-7 (NLT) *Love is patient and kind. Love is not jealous or boastful or proud 5 or rude. It does not demand its own way. It is not irritable, and it keeps no record of being wronged. 6 It does not rejoice about injustice but rejoices whenever the truth wins out. 7 Love never gives up, never loses faith, is always hopeful, and endures through every circumstance.*

2. Be very sensitive to all of this scripture when operating in the gifts of the Spirit.
3. Proper use of the gifts of the spirit is never self-serving.
4. Each gift becomes practically useless when used without love.
5. As we seek to identify and utilize the gifts God has given to us, we should make loving God, and loving each other, our highest motivation and priority.

B. SECOND KEY – AUTHORITY

> Isaiah 22:22 (NLT) *I will give him the key to the house of David – the highest position in the royal court. When he opens doors, no one will be able to close them; when he closes doors, no one will be able to open them.*

First, I would definitely say that all authority begins with God; there is no authority except from Him.

1. Authority refers to power.
2. Authority refers to ability.
3. Authority refers to capability.
4. Authority also refers to having been given authorization.

Key Point: We access God-given authority by believing in the name of Jesus and trusting in the Holy Spirit's power to accomplish our God-given purpose.

> Ephesians 1:21-22 (NLT) *Now he is far above any ruler or authority or power or leader or anything else – not only in this world but also in the world to come.* **22** *God has put all things under the authority of Christ and has made him head over all things for the benefit of the church.*

> Matthew 28:18 (NLT) *Jesus came and told his disciples, "I have been given all authority in heaven and on earth."*

Having access to the gifts of the Spirit requires us to stay in constant fellowship with and partnering with Jesus, as our friend, and confidant. Your adoration and love for Him must be first and foremost.

SESSION 7: The Keys to the Kingdom

C. THIRD KEY – FAITH

> Hebrews 11:5 (NLT) *It was by faith that Enoch was taken up to heaven without dying – "he disappeared because God took him." For before he was taken up, he was known as a person who pleased God.*

> Hebrews 11:6 (NLT) *And it is impossible to please God without faith. Anyone who wants to come to him must believe that God exists and that he rewards those who sincerely seek him.*

Key Point: Faith is when you can't see God's plan, but you trust in His Outcome.

> 1 Peter 1:4-7 (NLT) *and we have a priceless inheritance – an inheritance that is kept in heaven for you, pure and undefiled, beyond the reach of change and decay. 5 And through your faith, God is protecting you by his power until you receive this salvation, which is ready to be revealed on the last day for all to see. 6 So be truly glad. There is wonderful joy ahead, even though you must endure many trials for a little while. 7 These trials will show that your faith is genuine. It is being tested as fire tests and purifies gold – though your faith is far more precious than mere gold. So when your faith remains strong through many trials, it will bring you much praise and glory and honor on the day when Jesus Christ is revealed to the whole world.*

1. True faith changes the heart. Real faith seeks peace, having been saved by justifying faith.
2. Every believer should put their trust in Him alone by believing His word and living by faith, and diligently seeking His face day by day.
3. Faith should also start with believing in His truth, He is who He is.
4. Faith combines assurance, promises, and anticipation that our confidence and our hope, based on past experiences, that freshly surprise us, shall surely be ours. If He said it, we should believe it!
5. Our faith in God will grow much more as we love God in times of our trials.
6. As we dedicate our lives to Him.
7. As we genuinely love others.
8. As we are growing in Christian, Godly, character.

Operating in these Godly characteristics will please our God. As a last important point on faith – Believing and trusting in Jesus and reaching out to accept His wonderful gift of salvation is by faith in Him alone.

D. FOURTH KEY – OBEDIENCE

Deuteronomy 5:33 (NLT) *Stay on the path that the Lord your God has commanded you to follow. Then you will live long and prosperous lives in the land you are about to enter and occupy.*

SESSION 7: The Keys to the Kingdom

> Revelation 3:10-11 (NLT) *Because you have obeyed my command to persevere, I will protect you from the great time of testing that will come upon the whole world to test those who belong to this world. 11 I am coming soon..."*

> John 14:15 (NLT) *"If you love me, obey my commandments."*

> Deuteronomy 28:9 (NLT) *If you obey the commands of the Lord your God and walk in his ways, the Lord will establish you as his holy people as he swore he would do.*

> Deuteronomy 5:33 (NLT) *Stay on the path that the Lord your God has commanded you to follow. Then you will live long and prosperous lives in the land you are about to occupy.*

Key Point: Obedience is a gift.

How it benefits us, is that it frees us to receive what God gives and promises. He wants to bless us with His promises. Something so infinitely better than anything we already have, which is Himself!

Some of the blessings of walking in obedience to God:

a. We receive freedom from spiritual bondage.

b. We receive personal growth from the Holy Spirit.

c. We receive protection from danger, often He warns us beforehand.

d. Obedience being joy.

e. Obedience gives us hope. For example, obedience to God in our daily walk is key to unlocking to gifts of the Spirit that God has given to us, and our ability to be obedient as the Holy Spirit prompts you to prophesy or to pray and lay hands on the sick, as He directs.

f. Ultimately, obedience leads to a life in the presence of the Heavenly Father.

E. FIFTH KEY – PURPOSE

Revelation 3:12 (NLT) *All who are victorious will become pillars in the Temple of my God, and they will never have to leave it. And I will write on them the name of my God, and they will be citizens in the city of my God – the new Jerusalem that comes down from heaven from my God. And I will also write on them my new name.*

Notice - everything will be pure and new, for those whose name is written in the Lamb's Book of Life (the list of the redeemed).

Romans 8:28 (NKJV) *Romans 8:28 (NKJV) And we know that all things work together for good to those who love God, to those who are the called according to His purpose.*

Ephesians 3:10 (NKJV) *God's purpose in all this was to use the church to display his wisdom in its rich variety to all the unseen rulers and authorities in the heavenly places.*

KEY POINT: Let us for a moment align our thoughts with the realm of Heaven through salvation, which is the generous gift from God

SESSION 7: The Keys to the Kingdom

accomplished through His son Jesus. This led to a bridge of eternal purpose that we are destined for God's authentic plan. In this process there are many gifts He has given us to accomplish His purpose says God in your destiny and calling. This key unlocks many amazing possibilities that He has in store for His people. He works powerfully and creatively in us. This scripture points to us being His masterpiece. As we operate in the spiritual gifts that He has given to us He calls us to honor one another, as part of His care, for each of us. As God uses you to accomplish His purpose you are a beautiful canvas upon which He is painting His masterpiece.

> Jeremiah 29:11 (NLT) *"For I know the plans I have for you," says the Lord. "They are plans for good and not for disaster, to give you a future and a hope."*

God offers a fresh start at a new spiritual life. Let's go in Jesus' name.

F. SIXTH KEY – GRACE

> 2 Corinthians 12:8-9 (NLT) *Three different times I begged the Lord to take it away. 9 Each time he said, "My grace is all you need. My power works best in weakness." So now I am glad to boast about my weaknesses, so that the power of Christ can work through me.*

KEY POINT: By grace we obtain and surrender to salvation, recognizing that salvation is a gift from God to save us from our sin. And we are given a new spiritual life forever in Heaven. And then He gives us even more spiritual gifts to serve God and others, and it is these spiritual gifts that set us apart.

> Romans 12:6 (NLT) *In his grace, God has given us different gifts for doing certain things well. So if God has given you the ability to prophesy, speak out with as much faith as God has given you.*

In grace, God shows Himself to be a giver. God wants us to use these gifts in accordance with our faith. Use this key with humility. Don't think of yourself more highly than you ought. Don't allow yourself to be sinfully self-serving. If you do you will be cheating God and cheating others as well as yourself.

> Romans 12:3 (NLT) *Because of the privilege and authority God has given to me, I give each of you this warning: Don't think you are better than you really are. Be honest in your evaluation of yourselves, measuring yourselves by the faith God has given us.*

A key point is that God's gifts of grace are His undeserved love toward us, and therefore, God graces us with gifts.

    a. We must realize that all gifts and abilities come from God.

    b. Understand that not everyone has the same gift.

    c. Dedicate our gift(s) to God's service and not to our personal success.

    d. Be willing to use our gifts wholeheartedly, not holding back anything from God Himself or His service to serve others.

> e. Our goal or our chief role should be to observe ways to serve others. Building up the Church is vital to God.

Grace can only be accepted in thankfulness and praise. Grace cannot be earned at all!

G. SEVENTH KEY – HUMILITY

Matthew 23:11-12 (NLT) *The greatest among you must be a servant.* 12 *But those who exalt themselves will be humbled, and those who humble themselves will be exalted.*

KEY POINT: Jesus says that there is no higher calling than to be a servant. Jesus Christ was and is the greatest model of walking in humility because as the King that He was and is he could have demanded to be served, but as we read the scriptures, we come to know Him as a true servant in all aspects of His life. It wasn't important how people saw Him, in terms of His image, but how He saw people. He served the rich and the poor and lowly, and He displayed this characteristic as well! And remember He did this as King. It's not about how you wear your godly character, it's how that character fits you in serving God. More than wearing a godly image it is having a godly character.

When we operate in Spiritual Gifts let us honor God with a servant's heart, by demonstrating the attitude and motivation of intention to serve one another, operating in purity of heart by desiring the most effective purpose while focusing on the body of Christ. And purposefully building up one another with sincerity and love, gentleness, and peace. Jesus valued others' well-being above that of Himself.

Philippians 2:3-8 (NKJV) Let nothing be done through selfish ambition or conceit, but in lowliness of mind let each esteem others better than himself. 4 let each of you look out not only for his own interests, but also for the interests of others. 5 Let this mind be in you which was also in Christ Jesus, 6 who, being in the form of God, did not consider it robbery to be equal with God, but made Himself of no reputation, taking the form of a bondservant, and coming in the likeness of men. 8 And being found in appearance as a man, he humbled Himself and became obedient to the point of death, even the death of the cross.

- **WHAT ACTIVATES THE KEY'S TO THE KINGDOM?**

KEY POINT: Activating the gifts requires faith and grace as well as spiritual maturity. Spiritual maturity is defined by the fruit of the Spirit that emulates the character of Christ. When Christ controls us, these fruits grow in us naturally. We must live in close union with Jesus. As a result, we can love God and live in perfect harmony with the Law.

Hearing truth and gaining understanding deepens our love toward God, and reverence for God assures us to have the mind of Christ. And this gives us insight which is beyond our natural human ability and the attitude of Christ. There are hindrances to our stepping into the truth.

   a. A spirit of stubbornness, unwilling to accept the truth when heard.

   b. A lukewarmness for the things of God, lowering the passion or hunger for truth.

SESSION 7: The Keys to the Kingdom

Allowing God to place in us as believers a love and respect for the Word of God sets our conscious mind free.

H. FAITH

Faith is the activator and way into the spirit realm when accompanied by reason of use.

> Matthew 9:20-22 (NKJV) *And suddenly, a woman who had a flow of blood for twelve years came from behind and touched the hem of His garment. 21 For she said to herself, "If only I may touch His garment, I shall be made well." 22 But Jesus turned around, and when He saw her He said, "Be of good cheer, daughter; your faith has made you well." And the woman was made well from that hour.*

I. THE HEART OF GOD VS. THE HEART OF THE INNER MAN

It is God's divine faith and heart that enables us to act, decide, and do. The focus of our faith should primarily be motivated with the right heart of purity and belief and trust in Christ through the power of the Holy Spirit. Not ever trusting the heart of the inner man (self). Meaning that it is vital to have a relationship with God just as Jesus did have with His Father.

> John 5:17 (NLT) *But Jesus replied, "My Father is always working, and so am I."*

> John 5:19-20 (NLT) *So Jesus explained, "I tell you the truth, the Son can do nothing by himself. He does only what he*

sees the Father doing. Whatever the Father does, the Son also does. 20 For the Father loves the Son and shows him everything he is doing. In fact, the Father will show him how to do even greater works than healing this man. Then you will truly be astonished.

J. FAITHFULNESS AND JOY

Faithfulness is a fruit of the Spirit and joy that brings more than a feeling; it is a powerful emotion (as opposed to merely a feeling).

It is:
1. Fruit of faithfulness in trustworthiness
2. Quiet and steady
3. Unwavering in trust in the goodness of God
4. Wisdom and faithfulness in God

Romans 5:2 (NLT) *Because of our faith, Christ has brought us into this place of undeserved privilege where we now stand, and we confidently and joyfully look forward to sharing God's glory.*

Romans 5:1 (NLT) *Therefore, since we have been made right in God's sight by faith, we have peace with God because of what Jesus Christ our Lord has done for us.*

Philippians 4:6-7 (NLT) *Don't worry about anything; instead, pray about everything. Tell God what you need and thank him for all he has done. 7 Then you will experience God's peace, which exceeds anything we can understand. His peace will guard your hearts and minds as you live in Christ Jesus.*

SESSION 7: The Keys to the Kingdom

SPIRITUAL GIFTS

Session 8: WHY IS PROPHECY FOR TODAY?

Key Verse: 1 Corinthians 14:3 (NLT)
3 But one who prophesies strengthens others, encourages them, and comforts them.

The Purpose: It is scripturally wise to understand the importance and value of this gift. God uses this gift to speak through others to His Church, for the purpose of strengthening as well as bringing comfort, hope, and peace to the Body. We need to yield full cooperation with the Holy Spirit, fully embrace the excitement of we believers that desire to commune with God as we can and will hear Him speak through His people. So many Christians deny this important part of scripture that denotes intimacy. Because how do you hear from someone you don't know? This is a challenge for a lot of Christians, and they are missing out of so much that they would have by dialoging with God. He is extremely relational.

A. THE OFFICE OF THE PROPHET

> Jeremiah 1:5 (NLT) *"I knew you before I formed you in your mother's womb. Before you were born I set you apart and appointed you as my prophet to the nations."*

A prophet is a person whom God chooses before birth. It is a "calling" and you are chosen to be a mouthpiece for God, just as Jeremiah was. No man can birth this in you, only God. This way He decides His purpose

SESSION 8: Why is Prophecy for Today?

and determines how He will use you. He or she will carry the following characteristics:

   a. Bring people to repentance, to turn from their sin.

   b. Warn people of their idolatry.

   c. Bring correction or redirection.

   d. Lead people to God, or back to Him as their first love.

   e. A prophet also receives revelation, and words of wisdom from the heavenly counsel of God as he consistently stays in direct communion with God, through prayer, intercession, and worship.

The office of the Prophet is a gift extension of Jesus Christ, Himself as "The Prophet." Jesus was in Himself the full expression of all of the "five-fold" ministry giftings.

1. **Jesus the Apostle** – Hebrews 3:1 (NLT) And so, dear brothers and sisters who belong to God and are partners with those called to heaven, think carefully about this Jesus whom we declare to be God's messenger and High Priest.

2. **Jesus the Prophet** – Acts 3:22 (NLT) Moses said, "The Lord your God will raise up for you a Prophet like me from among your own people. Listen carefully to everything he tells you."

3. **Jesus the Evangelist** – Matthew 4:23 (NLT) Jesus traveled throughout the region of Galilee, teaching in the

synagogues and announcing the Good News about the Kingdom. And he healed every kind of disease and illness.

4. **Jesus the Pastor** – John 10:14 (NLT) "I am the good shepherd; I know my own sheep, and they know me, just as my Father knows me and I know the Father. So, I sacrifice my life for the sheep.

5. **Jesus the Teacher** – John 3:2 After dark one evening, he came to speak with Jesus. "Rabbi," he said, "we all know that God has sent you to teach us. Your miraculous signs are evidence that God is with you."

B. THE OFFICE OF A PROPHET – A HIGHER CALLING THAN THE GIFT OF PROPHECY

Prophets walk, in the calling of God to specifically take strong stands in walking in governmental authority. They are expected to walk with higher authority that is beyond that of exercising the gift of prophecy. It is a calling because God calls it from the womb.

> Isaiah 6:6-8 (NKJV) *Then one of the seraphim flew to me with a burning coal he had taken from the altar with a pair of tongs. 7 He touched my lips with it and said, "See, this coal has touched your lips. Now your guilt is removed, and your sins are forgiven." 8 Then I heard the Lord asking, "Whom should I send as a messenger to this people? Who will go for us?" I said, "Here I am. Send me."*

> Isaiah 49:1-2 (NLT) *Listen to me, all you in distant lands! Pay attention, you who are far away! The Lord called me*

SESSION 8: Why is Prophecy for Today?

> *before my birth; from within the womb he called me by name. 2 He made my words of judgment as sharp as a sword. he has hidden me in the shadow of his hand. I am like a sharp arrow in his quiver.*

The office of the Prophet is a calling by God from within the womb for the purpose of:

1. Prophets flow in areas of guidance, instruction, judgments, and rebukes concerning revelations given to the church by Christ for the purpose of purification and perfecting the Church.

2. Prophets are also given special abilities to know God's gifts and callings in a person's life, and to activate saints into their portion of the work of the ministry, to train and equip the body and govern.

3. The Prophet is called by God first, from within the womb and may be affirmed by other five-fold ministries, or ministers.

4. God chooses the Prophet for the office. It is not a choice made by man and the calling is for life.

5. Functions of the Prophet outlined in scripture included:

    b. **Giving Corrections** – Ezekiel 3:18 (NLT) "If I warn the wicked, 'saying you are under the penalty of death', but you fail to deliver the warning, they will die in their sins. And I will hold you responsible for their deaths."

    c. **Providing Direction** – 1 Kings 22:7 (NLT) But Jehoshaphat asked, "Is there not also a prophet of the Lord here? We should ask him the same question." (and) 2 Kings 5:10 (NLT) But Elisha sent a messenger out to him with his message: "Go and wash yourself seven times in the Jordan River. Then your skin will be restored, and you will be healed of your leprosy."

d. **Laying Foundations in the Church** – Ephesians 2:20 (NLT) Together we are his house, built on the foundation of the apostles and the prophets. And the cornerstone is Christ Jesus himself.

e. **Imparting Spiritual Gifts** – 1 Timothy 4:14 (NLT) Do not neglect the spiritual gift you received through the prophecy spoken over you when the elders of the church laid their hands on you.

Stirring up, challenging, and bringing saints out of dormancy to move forward by the word of the Lord. Just as Haggai stirred up the builders and people who then said, "we must build His house." (Haggai 1:2-10 NLT).

D. PROPHETIC PREACHING

Ezekiel 37:15-19 (NLT) *Again a message came to me from the Lord:* **16** *"Son of man, take a piece of wood and carve on it these words: 'This represents Judah and its allied tribes.' Then take another piece and carve these words on it: 'This represents Ephraim and the northern tribes of Israel.'* **17** *Now hold them together in your hand as if they were one piece of wood.* **18** *When your people ask you what your actions mean,* **19** *say to them, 'This is what the Sovereign Lord says: I will take Ephraim and the northern tribes and join them to Judah. I will make them one piece of wood in my hand.'*

Preaching biblical truth from the Word, because God said it, as the preacher yields to the fullness of the five-fold ministry. The prophetic ministry offers hope and inspiration.

c. Under the unction of God, and Holy Spirit-directed prophetic preaching often includes the use of illustrative demonstration material or visual aides to assist people with receiving God's point in the message on one level. At the same time on a deeper level Holy Spirit releases prophetic language inside of the preached message bringing clarity, direction, and divine wisdom beyond that which the preacher otherwise would have been able to release through the message on their own.

d. Ezekiel 4:4 (NLT) "Then lie on your side and put the sin of the people of Israel upon yourself. You are to bear their sin for the number of days you lie on your side.

e. Any five-fold minister can function in prophetic preaching at the direction of the Word.

I have witnessed this in various churches and those in attendance were so excited, and at that moment they did experience to a much greater degree that the preached Word of God is alive with application, more clarity reaching further into their mind and their heart. I love God and His creative nature.

SPIRITUAL GIFTS

D. PROPHETIC PRESBYTERY

The Presbytery is the gathering of people who have the authority to govern over churches in matters of doctrine and Pastoral appointment of clergy within the local church.

1 Timothy 4:14 (NLT) *Do not neglect the spiritual gift you received through the prophecy spoken over you when the elders of the church laid their hands on you.*

1. The Prophetic Presbytery is a gathering of "proven" ministers and elders, largely who function in the five-fold ministries.

2. Also functioning as prophetic servants, prophetic worship, prophetic intercession, and raising up prophetic teams, by reason of use.

3. The five-fold ministers should be available and active in the church today, bringing strength to the body of Christ, by reason of use.

4. Teaching, training, and activating the church today.

5. Bringing prophetic revelation and confirmation of those called to leadership in the church. They should always be Holy Spirit-led, just as Barnabas and Saul.

    a. Acts 13:1-3 (NLT) Among the prophets and teachers of the church at Antioch of Syria were Barnabas, Simeon (called "the black man"), Lucius (from Cyrene), Manaen (the childhood companion of King Herod Antipas), and Saul. 2 One day as these men were worshiping the Lord and fasting, the Holy Spirit said, "Appoint Barnabas and Saul for the special work to which I have called them." 3 So after more fasting and prayer, the men laid their hands on them and sent them on their way.

6. To urge every believer to progress in Christian maturity.

    a. Ephesians 4:11-13 (NLT) Now these are the gifts Christ gave to the church: the apostles, the prophets, the evangelists, and the pastors and teachers. 12 Their responsibility is to equip God's people to do his work and build up the church, the body of Christ. 13 This will continue until we all come to such unity in our faith and knowledge of God's son that we will be mature in the Lord, measuring up to the full and complete standard of Christ.

7. Ordination to the five-fold ministry.

    a. Titus 1:5 (NLT) I left you on the island of Crete so you could complete our work there and appoint elders in each town as I instructed you.

Here Paul entrusted Titus to lead the church in Crete. He recognized Titus' leadership abilities and urged him to use his abilities well. Elders must not just teach the word but live it. Most of God's qualifications require character over knowledge or skill.

E. THE GIFT OF PROPHECY

The gift of prophecy is a "GIFT", not an "OFFICE".

SPIRITUAL GIFTS

> *1 Corinthians 14:3 (NLT) But one who prophesies strengthens others, encourages them, and comforts them.*

1. It is a gift of the Holy Spirit.

2. It is received by grace through faith.

   a. *Romans 12:6 (NLT) In his grace, God has given us different gifts for doing certain things well. So if God has given you the ability to prophesy, speak out with as much faith as God has given you.*

   b. *Galatians 3:5 (NLT) I ask you again, does God give you the Holy Spirit and work miracles among you because you obey the law? Of course not! It is because you believe the message you heard about Christ.*

3. It is not based on human knowledge but incorrect doctrine will hinder it.

   1. *Acts 19:1-6 (NLT) While Apollos was in Corinth, Paul traveled through the interior regions until he reached Ephesus, on the coast, where he found several believers. 2 "Did you receive the Holy Spirit when you believed?" he asked them. "No," they replied, "We haven't even heard that there is a Holy Spirit." 3 "Then what baptism did you experience?" he asked. And they replied, "The baptism of John." 4 Paul said, "John's baptism called for repentance from sin. But John himself told the people to believe in the one who would come later, meaning Jesus." 5 As soon as they heard this, they were baptized in the name of the Lord Jesus. 6 Then where Paul laid his hands on them, the Holy*

SESSION 8: Why is Prophecy for Today?

> *Spirit came on them, and they spoke in other tongues and prophesied.*

4. It cannot be earned.

   a. *1 Corinthians 4:7 (NLT) For what gives you the right to make such a judgment? What do you have that God hasn't given you? And if everything you have is from God, why boast as though it were not a gift?*

5. It is not based on Christian maturity.

   a. *Acts 10:45 (NLT) The Jewish believers who came with Peter were amazed that the gift of the Holy Spirit had been poured out on the Gentiles, too.*

   b. *James 1:17-18 (NLT) Whatever is good and perfect is a gift coming down to us from God our Father, who created all the lights in the heavens. He never changes or casts a shifting shadow. 18 He chose to give birth to us by giving us his true word. And we, out of all creation, became his prized possession.*

As a person operates in their gift he or she is defined as a saint doing the work of the ministry. It is a gift of life from God.

F. THE IMPORTANCE OF PROPHECY

1 Thessalonians 5:19-22 (NLT) Do not stifle the Holy Spirit. 20 Do not scoff at prophecies, 21 but test everything that is said. Hold on to what is good. 22 Stay away from every kind of evil.

1. Concerning verse 19, God has often spoken through His Prophets, and some still beg to differ. We should not stifle the Holy Spirit. We shouldn't ignore or toss aside the gifts of the Holy Spirit. Often times spiritual gifts are very controversial. Rather than talk to God about this some just smother the gifts, and this is prevalent in a lot of churches. This is why some churches are "dead". We should not stifle the Holy Spirit in anyone's life, but we should encourage the full expression of His gifts to benefit the whole body of Christ.

2. In verses 20 and 21 it continues that we shouldn't make fun of those with whom we don't agree concerning the belief in prophesy, which is referred to as scoffing. But we should always test everything that is said by checking their word compared with the Bible. We offend God and it is dangerous ground we are on if we laugh at a person who speaks God's truth, through the gift of prophecy.

3. The gift is less about future events than about bringing messages from God, under the direction of the Holy Spirit to the body of believers. More Christians should see this gift today. On the one hand, prophecies should not be ignored at all. People who ignore Prophets or prophecies might as well ignore God as if His voice does not exist. God graces His people with this gift out of love for His people, to yield correction, warning, insight, and encouragement.

4. This gift that God gives to us should bring conviction by the Holy Spirit. The Holy Spirit convicts us as to what God wants, warning us to flee from temptation, and helping us discern truth. Ignoring these inner promptings quenches Him in our everyday lives. And not acting on these spiritual gifts can hinder God's work at a particular place and time. "Trust in the Lord" and use your gifts.

5. If someone prophecies in a foreign language there must be other mature prophets present in the atmosphere to interpret the prophetic word so all who are present will benefit.

G. WHY IS PROPHECY FOR TODAY?

Because God is still speaking today. He has never stopped since the beginning of creation. The question is, are we "listening?"

Romans 12:6 (NLT) *In his grace, God has given us different gifts for doing certain things well. So if God has given you the ability to prophesy, speak out with as much faith as God has given you.*

1 Corinthians 14:31 (NLT) *In this way, all who prophesy will have a turn to speak, one after the other, so that everyone will learn and be encouraged.*

- **When is there a prophetic atmosphere?**

    1. When the Spirit of prophecy is present (and any believer can enter in and exercise faith to prophesy).

Let us prophesy according to the proportion of faith God has given to each of us by His grace.

2. When Pastors and other five-fold ministers willingly operate as God appoints, allowing the Holy Spirit to bring comfort, edification, encouragement, and exhortation through Prophets and also through believers a prophetic atmosphere exists. They MUST agree wholeheartedly and fully trust the Holy Spirit, and not fear man. And remember, it is about how God wants to mature his Bride, for the bridegroom.

> Revelation 22:1 (NLT) *Then the angel showed me a river with the water of life, clear as crystal, flowing from the throne of God and of the Lamb.*

> Revelation 22:17 (NLT) *The Spirit and the bride say, "Come." Let anyone who hears this say, "Come." Let anyone who is thirsty come. Let anyone who desires drink freely from the water of life.*

3. Church leaders have to be willing to allow the manifestation of the expression of the gifts, as God directs so that everyone can participate in the building up of God's Church. The leaders must be sensitive and responsive to the Holy Spirit as He administers His gifting in church services, as He expresses Himself through His gifts, in this case through prophecy and through all the other amazing gifts God has willed and purposed for all believers.

SESSION 8: Why is Prophecy for Today?

    a. When a mighty prophetic presence of the Lord permeates the atmosphere making it easier to prophesy than to keep silent.

    b. When people come into the company of a Prophet or under the mantle of a senior or seasoned anointed Prophet.

    c. When the people are challenged by a minister to let God arise and testify through them by the Spirit of Prophesy.

Everything points back to Jesus, always victorious over all things. I want to be invited to the wedding, Amen.

Revelation 19:10 (NLT) *Then I fell down at his feet to worship him, but he said, "No don't worship me. I am a servant of God, just like you and your brothers and sisters who testify about their faith in Jesus. Worship only God. For the essence of prophecy is to give a clear witness for Jesus."* In the King James version, it reads in part, "For the testimony of Jesus is the spirit of prophecy."

Read the following additional scriptures for more examples of the Spirit of Prophecy:

- Numbers 11:24-29
- Numbers 12:5-6
- Deuteronomy 18:15-22
- Deuteronomy 13:1-5
- 1 Samuel 10:10
- 1 Samuel 19:20-24

Session 9: DEVELOPING PROPHETIC TEAMS

Key Verse: Ephesians 2:19 (NLT)
19 So now you Gentiles are no longer strangers and foreigners. You are citizens along with all of God's holy people. You are members of God's family.

The Purpose: To establish a team in the spirit with the heart "mentality" of a team of co-laborers for the Kingdom of God. Team ministry is important to God for harmony with each other in the body especially concerning the gifts of the Spirit, and most importantly concerning the prophetic voice of God. Always in unity of mindfulness of who He is in the hearing and speaking prophecy. Let's check into and lay the scriptural foundation and benefits of team ministry. I believe God wants and desires that we operate effectively in this area. As we do so we will be more astute with increasing clarity and become greater at reproducing effective work for the Kingdom of God. An example; I recall an awesome experience when after I graduated from the School of Prophets so much power and strength in the many like-minded students working in such harmony. For our first assignment, we traveled to a Church and prophesied to over 300 saints and God moved powerfully!

A. THE TRINITY IS VITAL

The Godhead is composed of three separate personalities in perfect union. God the Father, His Son, and the Holy Spirit. This is part of the divine nature of God. Each is eternal, possessing a distinct personality, revealing supernatural omniscience, will, and emotion.

SESSION 9: Developing Prophetic Teams

>Colossians 2:9 (NLT) *For in Christ lives all the fullness of God in a human body.*

1. Christ alone holds all the answers to the true meaning of life because He is "LIFE".
   2. Christ is the unique source of knowledge and power for Christian life.

While the Godhead is much more than this, our concept of team and our best role model of team is in the Godhead. We see this in the creation of the world.

>John 1:1-3 (NLT) *In the beginning the Word already existed. The Word was with God, and the Word was God. 2 He existed in the beginning with God. 3 God created everything through him, and nothing was created except through him.*

>Matthew 28:19 (NLT) *Therefore, go and make disciples of all the nations, baptizing them in the name of the Father, and the Son and the Holy Spirit.*

1. The Father draws sinners: John 6:44 (NLT) For no one can come to me unless the Father who sent me draws them to me, and at the last day I will raise them up.

2. The Holy Spirit convicts: John 16:8 (NLT) And when he comes, he will convict the world of its sin, and of God's righteousness, and of the coming judgment.

3. The Son Saves: Romans 10:13 (NLT) For "Everyone who calls on the name of the Lord will be saved."

B. BENEFITS OF TEAM MINISTRY

SPIRITUAL GIFTS

1 Peter 4:10 (NLT) God has given each of you a gift from his great variety of spiritual gifts. Use them well to serve one another.

Just as the trinity has benefitted us enormously, as true believers we have experienced true salvation, resurrection, and revelation.

Teamwork increases effectiveness and reproduction for sure! There is more fruit with greater multiplication. Team ministry is a group of people who are laboring (action) together (unity) in an organized way (order) to accomplish a common (purpose). Teams can be defined as:

1. To yoke together
2. Working together in an orderly fashion
3. To join in together in activity (action)

Ecclesiastes 4:9-12 (NLT) Two people are better off than one, for they can help each other succeed. 10 If one person falls, the other can reach out and help. But someone who falls alone is in real trouble. 11 Likewise, two people lying close together can keep each other warm. But how can one be warm alone? 12 A person standing alone can be attacked and defeated, but two can stand back-to-back and conquer. Three are even better for a triple-braided cord is not easily broken.

1. **Provision**: Abilities joined, creativity, effectiveness, sharpness, and multiplication
2. **Security**: Not by self, someone to turn to, a higher authority or father
3. **Comfort**: Compatibility, confirmation, encouragement
4. **Protection**: As in from false accusation

SESSION 9: Developing Prophetic Teams

5. **Strength**: A threefold cord is not quickly "broken", tremendous increase

Folks, let go of the spirit of independence. Being independent is not the way to your destiny in Christ.

- **More Benefits of Team Ministry:** Depending on Christ's ultimate benefit.

    Proverbs 11:14 (NLT) *Without wise leadership, a nation falls; there is safety in having many advisers.*

1. Team ministry brings safety and balance. A good leader needs and uses wise advisors. One person's perspective and understanding is severely limited.

2. It lightens one's load and takes the pressure off. No one has to do it all. It provides shared ownership, order, and AUTHORITY.

3. *Mark 6:7 (NLT) And he called his twelve disciples together and began sending them out two by two, giving them authority to cast out evil spirits.* (He in this scripture is Jesus)

    a. They could strengthen and encourage each other.

    b. They could provide comfort and protection toward one another.

    c. They could sharpen each other's discernment and thereby make less mistakes.

    d. They could stir each other into action, a counter to idleness and indifference.

4. Our strength comes from God alone, but He meets His accomplishments through our cooperative teamwork with others.

C. WHY PROPHETIC TEAMS IN CHURCH?

Paul spoke extensively about the prophetic. His emphasis was in a plural manner, addressing that all should prophesy.

1) *1 Corinthians 14:24-25 (NLT) But if all of you are prophesying, and unbelievers or people who don't understand these things come into your meeting, they will be convicted or sin and judged by what you say. 25 As they listen, their secret thoughts will be exposed, and they will fall to their knees and worship God, declaring, "God is truly here among you."* – God uses prophesy in the Church to draw unbelievers to Jesus.

2) *1 Corinthians 14:29 (NLT) Let two or three people prophesy, and let the others evaluate what is said.* – Prophetic words are weighed by members of the prophetic team.

3) *1 Corinthians 14:27 (NLT) No more than two or three should speak in tongues. They must speak one at a time, and someone must interpret what they say.* – Sharp prophetic teams can weigh interpretations as well.

4) *Proverbs 27:17 (NLT) As iron sharpens iron, so a friend sharpens a friend.* – Every person gifted with prophecy needs to be sharpened.

SESSION 9: Developing Prophetic Teams

A Pastor can also be pastorally prophetic which is beautiful because it comes from the heart of a shepherd, and is soft, gentle, and caring. But when Pastors embrace it in their churches even though this is not their main calling it allows 90% of the impartation necessary for the whole church to benefit from the prophetic team. The Body of Christ operates through the Holy Spirit anointing all who host Him. I have witnessed as well as participated in an atmosphere of this capacity.

> Amos 3:7 (NLT) *Indeed, the sovereign LORD never does anything until he reveals his plans to his servants the prophets.*

The Lord is talking to Amos about revealing His plan not just to one prophet, but to several prophets, to a team of prophets. God never reveals His whole plan to one man alone. We also find that we can work as a team when we interpret dreams and visions. As we willingly participate with the Holy Spirit, we often find that we each have a part.

> 1 Corinthians 13:9 (KJV) *For we know in part, and we prophesy in part.*

We really and truly do need one another's knowledge and revelation. I believe the Church is being ripped off when it comes to the prophetic because so often a church will invite one Prophet to come and minister to them, and we lose the blessing that comes through prophetic teams. This should not be a "one-man show." Prophets raise up prophets, and the prophetic culture arises. God's heart wants this!

> Ecclesiastes 4:9 (NLT) *Two people are better off than one, for they can help each other succeed.*

Two prophets are better than one and three are better than two. What is better than two or three prophets? A pastor and a prophet, an evangelist and a prophet, a teacher and a prophet, or an apostle and a prophet. We need team players not just with other prophetic folks, but we need the five-fold ministries as well, as in Ephesians 4.

> Ephesians 4:11-13 (NLT) *Now these are the gifts Christ gave to the church: the apostles, the prophets, the evangelists, and the pastors and teachers. 12 Their responsibility is to equip God's people to do his work and build up the church, the body of Christ. 13 This will continue until we all come to such unity in our faith and knowledge of God's Son that we will be mature in the Lord.*

Prophetic Team is a powerful operation of biblical hope and encouragement. It is so powerful to work in unison with other ministries and there is safety when we work as a team and weigh each other's words. I live on the Central Coast in California, and I have to admit to a deprivation of this operation in this region. I ask why because I know that I should be in a place where prophets and the prophetic are welcome. Not just a select few, but God desires more not less. Let's choose to be a Team Player, Amen?

SESSION 9: Developing Prophetic Teams

Session 10: WHAT IS A PROPHETIC BURDEN

The Purpose: A burden that only God can give, and only God can enable to be carried, that can change a town, a city, a marriage, purpose, and destiny. Prophetic people carry this. Building a prophetic culture births Godly order. (Nehemiah 2:1-8 NLT)

1 Corinthians 14:39 (NLT) So, my dear brothers and sisters, be eager to prophesy, and don't forbid speaking in tongues.

Prophesy reveals the mind and heart of God, "one hundred percent", to His people and the main purpose is to draw His people closer to Himself, and to one another. It stimulates and encourages us to be better people before God. Prophecy encourages and comforts people and shows the tenderness of God when distress comes upon us.

1 Corinthians 12:7 (NLT) A spiritual gift is given to each of us so we can help each other.

Prophetic people should always be embraced within the church. These gifted people have always been shut down because they lack the communication skills and training, etiquette, or structure needed to make this gift profitable to the hearer. As a result, their prophetic words are messy and get them in trouble with their leaders. Equipping is necessary.

SESSION 10: What is a Prophetic Burden

1 Corinthians 14:31 (NLT) In this way, all who prophesy will have a turn to speak, one after the other, so that everyone will learn and be encouraged.

When team members take a risk, we need to celebrate them and guard them against perfectionism. Prophetic gifts grow in accuracy by taking risks. Prophetic culture, I really love this model. Use this gift outside the walls of the church in partnership with evangelism.

1 Corinthians 1:10 (NLT) I appeal to you, dear brothers and sisters, by the authority of our Lord Jesus Christ, to live in harmony with each other. Let there be no divisions in the church. Rather, be of one mind, united in thought and purpose.

A. New Model

1. Give a word of encouragement.
2. Give a correlating scripture.
3. Give the prophetic word.
4. Seal it with prayer and faith.

- **Consider the following whatever the model. (F A T S O)**

    1. Faithful – To God, putting God first.
    2. Available – To God, always.
    3. Teachable – From God, by the Holy Spirit.
    4. Spirit Led – By God, through the Holy Spirit.
    5. Obedient – To God, always.

B. Train and Keep Training:

1. Have a set training at least once per month.
2. Keep the training fresh and exciting.
3. Keep the team challenged and celebrate their victories.
4. The spirit of unity is vital.

C. Team Members need to understand:

1. Ability – The power of action.
2. Action – Steadfastness, diligence, and willingness to press into action.
3. Vision – The ability to see the strategy that accomplishes the team's purpose.
4. Spirit – The heart of the team, which is to emulate the spirit and heart of the kingdom.

Each team and each team member must have a love for the sheep more than a love for the position.

D. Evidence of the right spirit following Godly characteristics:

1. Meekness
2. Submission
3. Humility
4. Speaking into other's lives with transparency.

SESSION 10: What is a Prophetic Burden

E. A team member is supportive of their fellow team members and of leadership and grows in the following:

1. **Faithfulness**

    a. Willing to invest in other's ministry.

    b. Faithful to the vision of the house.

    c. A willing heart to train and serve.

2. **Humility**

    a. Preferring one another in love.

    b. Flexible in seeing other people's concepts, perspectives, or vision.

    c. Willing to receive correction/discipline.

3. **Loyalty**

    a. What we say – demonstrated by word.

    b. What we do – deed or action.

    c. What we convey – an attitude.

We can encourage one another's God-given talent by acknowledging and stirring God in each other. Then we excel beyond our own expectations.

Hallelujah!

Index:

activating the gifts (page 81) To use the gifts God has given to you. To receive God's grace to do it.

authority (page 72) The warranted right, power or ability to determine a thing in this case, walking in the gifts of the Spirit.

boldness (page 64) an attitude of strong confidence in God such that godly things are said and done openly without fear of consequences.

Bride (page 97) Experience Joys of God's invitation to all who thirst. The bride is the Church, who celebrate Him as we get equipped.

covet (page 10) To desire it for the cause of blessing others, not for personal gain.

enmity (page 28) Feeling actively hostile against God.

dialogue (page 3) This involves Him speaking and you listening or giving and receiving cultivates interaction.

discerning (page 25, 44) The ability to think biblically making careful distinctions between truth, lie, or error through the direction of the Holy Spirit to your spirit.

dulled (page 7) Being lazy and slothful or hard of hearing.

Godhead (page 101) Operating in the fullness of the Godhead. All three, Father, Son & Holy Spirit.

impressions (page 18, 22) An idea, sensed as a feeling about something or someone to bring hope or healing as in Isaiah 61:1 and often given by the Holy Spirit to convey a point.

intimacy (pages 3, 4, 10…) Closeness with God and close relationship with other people. an intimate quality or state.

manifold wisdom (page 39) The many facets of God's wisdom.

mantle (page 98) symbolic of a calling, ministry, or anointing when applicable to an office given to individuals by God, relating to the authority and importance.

presbytery (pages 90, 91) An assembly of elders in a church.

prophecy (page 87) A message from God and to prophesy is to speak or proclaim a message from God.

prophetic burdens (page 109) God's call to prayer and intercession for His assistance for you to perform and accomplish a task that He has given to you.

purpose (pages 1, 3, 4…) To serve God and others with His intentions.

realm (pages 15, 16…) The Kingdom of God which is where God reigns as King.

reformation (page 6) Choosing to allow the Holy Spirit to realign our lives with biblical values.

reprobate mind (page 29) One who rejects God or His gifts or having a seared consciousness.

revelation (page 35) Truths and knowledge that God has revealed for instruction and guidance.

scoff or scoffer (pages 8, 94) Someone who chooses to disbelieve God and His word. Someone who is arrogant and rejects the wisdom and God's truth found in the scriptures.

sheepfold (page 5) A protected place to keep the flock together.

soulish mind (pages 26, 27) The mind of a person with its own abilities relying on their own experience, stubborn and disobedient to God.

spirituality (page 1) God's holiness, gift of the spirit, life in the spirit. Quality of life, living under the control of the Holy Spirit.

supernatural (pages 1, 10, 15…) Above, beyond and far higher and greater than natural.

utterance (page 60) Relating to gifts of the Holy Spirit that have to do with speaking.

working of miracles (pages 63, and 64) To do the kind of amazing or wonderful thing that is only within the power of God.

My Personal Word for You:

As the Holy Spirit inspired me to put this manual together, I knew that the intended application was as a tool for collaboration of all of us who are in the Body of Christ, rather than as a book for personal enjoyment or individual edification alone. It was created for the purpose of allowing the Holy Spirit in all of us as believers to bring about the multiplication that only the collaboration within the Body of Christ affecting the Body of Christ or the Church to grow and mature into its full potential.

Folks, it takes an "army" of trained and equipped soldiers prepared for battle to raise up and build up one another for the purpose of fulfilling Ephesians 4:11, operating in the fullness of the gifts of the Spirit.

Activation takes place as we are like-minded, of the same spirit, in harmony with God first and then with one another. Activation is further accompanied by "reason of use". I recommend this training tool to first be used in small groups of Church Leaders to raise up and train others. Once like-minded trained and equipped leaders come together, I know that they can use this manual directly in small home groups in training others in the gifts of the Holy Spirit. Churches and ministries can use this material as part of a broader developed School of Ministry or School of the Prophets as examples of ways that this manual is designed to be useful in God's Kingdom.

May God anoint all who step into this place of enormous growth in maturity as The Bride matures and awaits the return of the Groom. Please raise up and train others. It is God's design and His desire. Let us see revival in our cities' churches.

In Christ,

Myra Armstrong
A Voice for God

Myra Armstrong Contact Info:

email: myraosuch@yahoo.com

phone: (805) 748-4957

www.ingramcontent.com/pod-product-compliance
Lightning Source LLC
Chambersburg PA
CBHW081156290426
44108CB00018B/2567